POPULATIO

The First Essay

POPULATION:
THE FIRST ESSAY

by
THOMAS ROBERT MALTHUS

with a Foreword by
Kenneth E. Boulding

ANN ARBOR PAPERBACKS
The University of Michigan Press

First edition as an Ann Arbor Paperback 1959
Foreword © by the University of Michigan 1959
Published in the United States of America by
the University of Michigan Press and simultaneously
in Toronto, Canada, by Ambassador Books, Ltd.

Manufactured in the United States of America

FOREWORD

by KENNETH E. BOULDING

It is no mean achievement in a book to inscribe its author's name on the languages of the world. Malthusian, Malthusianism, is a term understood in many languages, often with a somewhat opprobrious connotation. The reputation of Malthus, indeed, is one of the curious ironies of history. He was a kindly, gentle, sensitive, and sincere Christian minister, yet in many parts of the world his name stands for a cruel, mechanical doctrine of despair. He really knew very little about the theory of population and made no valuable original contributions to it, yet his name is ineradicably associated with the subject of population, so much so that one thinks of Malthus and population almost in the same breath. He was a great and insightful economist, yet for a hundred years his reputation as an economist rested on his essay on *Population* rather than on his economic writings proper, and the essay on *Population* is not a work in economics at all, but— especially the present edition—a work in moral philosophy and in the theory of history. In his later writing, especially in the great *Principles of Political Economy* and in his controversies with Ricardo, Malthus anticipates the employment theory of Keynes. This aspect of his work, however, was submerged for a whole century after his death. In the great controversy between Malthus and Ricardo—surely one of the most enlightened and least acrimonious controversies in history—Ricardo was left the undisputed master of the field until Keynes wrote in his delightful essay on Malthus, "if only Malthus, instead of Ricardo, had been the parent stem from which nineteenth-century economics proceeded, what a much wiser and richer place the world would be today!" (J. M. Keynes, *Essays in Biography* [New ed.; London, 1951], p. 120.)

To return, however, to the essay. Its history is well known. Thomas Robert Malthus was the son of modestly prosperous English landowner, Daniel Malthus, a man of liberal opinions and a friend of Rousseau. Father and son engaged in gentlemanly intellectual controversy. Daniel was an optimist, an admirer of

Godwin, and a great believer in the perfectibility of mankind. Son Robert, however, had read Adam Smith, and knew at least enough mathematics to be aware of the alarming powers of the geometrical progression. From Adam Smith he had learned the great concept of what now we would call equilibrium. An equilibrium population is a stationary population, and a stationary population is one in which the number of deaths is equal to the number of births in any given period of time. A population which is growing is not in equilibrium, but it cannot grow forever; at some time some kind of limit must be reached, and though equilibrium may be postponed, it cannot be postponed indefinitely. The limit which Robert had in mind was a limit imposed by the food supply. He supposed, as the strongest possible case, that the food supply might increase by a constant amount every year. This is the famous principle that food supply increases in arithmetic progression. In the first edition of the essay this is clearly only a "strong assumption"—a wildly optimistic assumption at that—and the whole purport of the argument is to show that even on this most optimistic assumption the geometric increase of population will soon outrun any conceivable increase in the food supply. In subsequent editions it would almost seem as if Malthus came to believe in the principle of arithmetic progression of the food supply as a "law," but his argument in no sense rests on it. The crucial principle is that there must be *some* limit to the number of mankind, and that growth of population, at no matter how slow a rate, must eventually bring the number to this limit. Even more dramatic illustrations of the power of growth at a constant rate can be devised than Malthus imagined. Thus, if the present world population of 2,500,000,000 people were to continue to grow at about its present rate of 2 per cent per annum, in only 765 years the whole surface of the earth (land and water) would be covered with a solid mass of people, and in a mere 8000 years the whole known astronomical universe, two thousand light years in radius, would be solid with humanity. Long before this time it is not unreasonable to postulate limits of the growth of population which will bring it to an equilibrium at a zero rate of growth.

The critical question is, of course, *what* is the ultimate limit on the growth of population. Suppose we start with a happy state of a relatively small population and abundant resources. The procreative powers being what they are, births—and what is more important, surviving births—exceed what is necessary to replace the population, and the population grows. It cannot, as we have seen, grow forever. What then, brings the growth to an end? Only two things, or a combination of them, can do this—declining fertility, or increasing mortality. Malthus is not hopeful about declining fertility. "Towards the extinction of the passion between the sexes, no progress whatever has hitherto been made." (Do we catch a slight twinkle in the clerical eye?) And for Malthus the link between what he so decorously calls the passion between the sexes and the growth of population is a strong one. But if fertility will not decline, the *only* method of reaching an equilibrium of population is by increasing mortality, and mortality is increased mainly through misery and starvation. Hence we get what I have elsewhere called the "Dismal Theorem": if the only ultimate check on the growth of population is misery, then the population will grow until it is miserable enough to stop its growth.

There is worse to come. There is what I have called the "Utterly Dismal Theorem," which states that any technical *improvement*, can only relieve misery for a while, for as long as misery is the only check on population the improvement will enable population to grow, and will soon merely enable *more* people to live in misery than before. The final result of improvements, therefore, is to increase the equilibrium population, which is to increase the total sum of human misery. It is little wonder that economics was called the "dismal science" and that even good father Daniel had his optimism somewhat shaken.

In the present essay the gloom is fairly unrelieved. There may be "preventive checks" which result from "foresight of the difficulties attending the rearing of a family" and hence which cut down fertility—even this, however, is conceived merely as a result of the contemplation of misery. More likely, we fear (though Malthus does not actually say so), are the "positive checks"—"the actual distresses of some of the lower classes, by which they are disabled from giving the proper food and attention to their children" and so infant mortality takes care of the excess of human fertility.

In all this there was nothing very new, as Malthus himself is the first to admit. Adam Smith and several earlier writers had made much the same point. What gave the essay on *Population* its extraordinary impact and makes it still well worth reading after more than a century and a half, is the eloquence and almost agonizing moral passion with which the theme is worked out, and the clear political conclusions, especially in regard to the Poor Law, which emerge from the argument. The essay is almost like a modern Book of Job. It is not that Malthus is personally afflicted—apart from the toothache in Chapter XII, which he clearly bears with fortitude and uses to illustrate (as against Godwin) the power of body over mind, Malthus was a singularly unafflicted person, living a calm, happy, and fruitful life. His affliction is an intellectual one—the contemplation of a system which seemed to promise man perpetual misery on earth, and to place him in the grip of implacable forces which no mere institutional changes could assuage. It is no wonder that the idealists and reformers, and even the Marxists with their grandiose vision of man in full control of his own society, have hated Malthus. Against all easy optimism he stands like a prophet of doom—reform society as you will, he seems to say, population will catch up with you; give all you can to the poor, and their poverty will not ultimately be relieved. Science and technical improvement, Christian love and generous impulses alike seem to be washed away down the stream of history on the awful flood of population.

Malthus is fully aware of the tragic nature of his system. He contemplates it with the horror which it deserves. Yet he is, after all, a Christian minister; he has an obligation to "justify God's ways to man." In his last eloquent chapter he offers what is a kind of evolutionary defense of God against the existence of "natural and moral evil," in which he argues that it is only the exertion to avoid evil which in the great course of time "forms matter into mind." His final paragraph begins, "Evil exists in the world, not to create despair, but activity." Here is the word of a young man who has had an appalling vision of almost unconquerable misery and yet who refuses to be ultimately daunted by it.

Looking back on this essay from the perspective of a hundred and sixty years, two aspects of it stand out which would not have been apparent to its first readers. We see it first as the harbinger of the Darwinian revolution in man's image of nature and himself. Darwin acknowledged a great debt to Malthus. The concept of ecological equilibrium, in which each species multiplies to the point where it reaches an equilibrium population, is a simple extension of the Malthusian system. The concept of evolution as ecological succession, in which small variations produce constant and irreversible changes in the equilibrium values of the populations of all species, is a simple extension of the notion of ecological equilibrium. In a sense therefore Malthus stands at the portal of the whole great movement of nineteenth-century evolutionary thought.

The other aspect of the backward look on the essay is the opportunity which it gives us to examine the Malthusian prophecies. In one country at least the Malthusian system operated ruthlessly in the nineteenth century. At the beginning of the eighteenth century Ireland had about two million people in it, living miserably for the most part on small grains. Then, in an early version of technical assistance, some benevolent improver introduced the potato, which produced much more food per acre than the previous crops. At first, of course, the Irish were substantially better fed. Better food, however, led to a decline in infant mortality, and the population began to rise rapidly. By 1845 there were eight million people, living about on the same level of misery on potatoes as the two million of a hundred and fifty years before. The improvement, in true dismal fashion, had just about quadrupled the amount of misery. Then came the blight, crop failure, and the famine. Two million starved to death, two million emigrated, leaving four million accommodated in modest comfort to the rather meager resources of the island. At this point the cycle should perhaps have started all over again, but it did not. The Irish had evidently learned a lesson, and the population has remained approximately constant at four million to this day—partly through continued emigration, but mainly through the advancement in the age of marriage, especially, of course, of women. It is striking that it is a Catholic country which has most successfully achieved population control!

In America, and indeed in the western world generally, the worst of the Malthusian prophecies have been postponed in spite of the great increase of population, first, by a large extension in the area of agricultural land, especially in America, South Africa, and Australasia, and second (in the last twenty-five years at least), by a remarkable rise in the yield of food per acre as a result of improved plants, such as hybrid corn, and the increased use of chemical fertilizer. It is a curious irony that in the western world, at least, food supply has more than kept pace with the growing population for more than a hundred and fifty years after Malthus who thought this might happen for twenty-five years, but for no longer. Because of this experience there has been a certain tendency to pooh-pooh the Malthusian specter as a pretty feeble ghost—after all, in a country which seems to have chronic agricultural surpluses the cry that population must eventually outrun food supply wears a little thin after a century and a half.

Nevertheless, the Malthusian specter is not easily laid. The Malthusian system, given the premises, is as irrefutable as a syllogism, and no amount of mere experience can stand up against a watertight logic. There is nothing in the Malthusian system which says that the attainment of the equilibrium population cannot be postponed; indeed, Malthus himself advocates devoting all possible energies to this, and lays great stress on the desirability of agricultural improvement. In the race between population and subsistence there may be quite long periods in which subsistence gains on population. *Eventually*, however, a stationary population *must* be reached on a limited earth or even in a limited universe. Then the critical question becomes what is the nature of this stationary equilibrium: is it an equilibrium with high birth rates and equally high death rates, or low birth rates and equally low death rates? The first is bound to be an equilibrium of misery, and worse than misery, of recurrent disaster, for the most likely form of this equilibrium is not one where deaths equal births every year, but where births exceed deaths for a while under temporarily easier conditions until the population rises to a number beyond the long run equilibrium, and it is eventually brought down again by famine, war, or pestilence. Only the second gives any ultimate promise of a stable, high-level society. We can argue on other grounds, of course, that we do not now have the techniques which would make a stable, high-level society possible—

that our high standard of living in the West is obtained only by squandering our geological capital or fuel and ores and that very soon (in a mere moment, in fact, in geological time) all our fuel and ore will be used up and we will have to revert to a much more primitive society, based almost entirely on the produce of field and forest. Atomic and solar energy, nitrogen from the air and magnesium from the sea give us at least the promise of a stable high-level technology, but even if we achieve this, we must still achieve population control. On this point the Malthusian logic is inescapable.

Fortunately, it is not too difficult to restate the Dismal Theorem in a moderately cheerful form, which states that if something else, other than misery and starvation, can be found which will keep a prosperous population in check, the population does not have to grow until it is miserable and starves, and can be stably prosperous. In the present essay Malthus is not optimistic about the "something else"—even his "preventive check" involves the contemplation of future misery—but in the second and subsequent editions (almost a totally different, and much duller work) he seems willing to extend the preventive check to the preservation of comfort rather than the contemplation of misery. How to do this, however, is a problem which so far has produced no wholly satisfactory solution. The Irish solution is clearly feasible, but at a high cost in frustration of the early delights of conjugal affection—a passion, which as the Reverend Malthus himself avers, is "not inconsistent either with reason or virtue." There is what might be called the Burmese solution, which is to encourage a large proportion of the population to enter monasteries and nunneries, but this is only a variant and institutionalization of the Irish solution. Contraception and planned parenthood, at least in the present state of knowledge and practice, is of dubious reliability; those who plan to have two children almost invariably end up with three, and three children per family in a high-level society without appreciable infant mortality produces a fatal rate of population increase. The sad truth is that although we know a lot more about the mathematics of population than Malthus did, we know very little more about its sociology. The debacle of the population experts in predicting the postwar population movements was spectacular and complete; the United States has already passed the population figure which the experts predicted in the early 1940's would be the stationary population of 1980, and the flood of births abates but slightly. We know very little about the subtle social—or even physical—forces which determine the crucial number of children per family. Until we do know more, the cheerful theorem remains with a question mark. Misery, we *know* will do the trick—this is the only sure-fire automatic method of bringing population to an equilibrium. Other things *may* do it. Malthus had a remarkable insight when he pointed out (Chapter II) that *room* as well as nourishment might limit natural populations. Robins, for instance, stake out a territory which yields them ample food supply and defend it valiantly, and a robin who cannot find a vacant territory, or cannot dispossess an existing tenant perishes. The prosperous appearance of the robin is a clear consequence of his territorial method of population control. Indeed, the species of the world of nature can fairly easily be divided into prosperous species which limit numbers by means other than food, and thin, starveling creatures who are limited by their food supply. Perhaps the best example is the prosperity of the house cat, whose numbers are limited strictly by the number of available catlovers, as against the miserable appearance of the alley cat whose numbers are limited by the food supply. The inference for the equilibrium of the human population is that there is much to be said for a housing shortage, and that equilibrium may well be achieved by limiting the number of nests and only allowing a new pair to set up housekeeping and propagation when an old pair has vacated.

All this is to show that Malthus (who, by the way, confined himself to three children, only one of which survived to maturity) is still worth reading, and still has important lessons for us today. The essay on *Population* is worth reading for its style and passion alone; this first edition is the first crow of a young cock, eloquent, passionate, alarming, awakening, unfootnoted, and eminently readable. It punctures the easy optimism of the utopians of any generation. But by revealing the nature of at least one dragon which must be slain before misery can be abolished, its ultimate message is one of hope, and the truth, however unpleasant, tends "not to create despair, but activity" of the right kind.

PREFACE

The following Essay owes its origin to a conversation with a friend, on the subject of Mr. Godwin's Essay, on avarice and profusion, in his Enquirer. The discussion started the general question of the future improvement of society; and the Author at first sat down with an intention of merely stating his thoughts to his friend, upon paper, in a clearer manner than he thought he could do in conversation. But as the subject opened upon him, some ideas occurred, which he did not recollect to have met with before; and as he conceived that every least light, on a topic so generally interesting, might be received with candour, he determined to put his thoughts in a form for publication.

The Essay might, undoubtedly, have been rendered much more complete by a collection of a greater number of facts in elucidation of the general argument. But a long and almost total interruption from very particular business, joined to a desire (perhaps imprudent) of not delaying the publication much beyond the time that he originally proposed, prevented the Author from giving to the subject an undivided attention. He presumes, however, that the facts which he has adduced will be found to form no inconsiderable evidence for the truth of his opinion respecting the future improvement of mankind. As the Author contemplates this opinion at present, little more appears to him to be necessary than a plain statement, in addition to the most cursory view of society, to establish it.

It is an obvious truth, which has been taken notice of by many writers, that population must always be kept down to the level of the means of subsistence; but no writer that the Author recollects has inquired particularly into the means by which this level is effected: and it is a view of these means which forms, to his mind, the strongest obstacle in the way to any very great future improvement of society. He hopes it will appear that, in the discussion of this interesting subject, he is actuated solely by a love of truth, and not by any prejudices against any particular set of men, or of opinions. He professes to have read some of the speculations on the future improvement of society in a temper very different from a wish to find them visionary, but he has not acquired that command over his understanding which would enable him to believe what he wishes, without evidence, or to refuse his assent to what might be unpleasing, when accompanied with evidence.

The view which he has given of human life has a melancholy hue, but he feels conscious, that he has drawn these dark tints, from a conviction that they are really in the picture, and not from a jaundiced eye or an inherent spleen of disposition. The theory of mind which he has sketched in the two last chapters accounts to his own understanding in a satisfactory manner for the existence of most of the evils of life, but whether it will have the same effect upon others must be left to the judgment of his readers.

If he should succeed in drawing the attention of more able men to what he conceives to be the principal difficulty in the way to the improvement of society and should, in consequence, see this difficulty removed, even in theory, he will gladly retract his present opinions and rejoice in a conviction of his error.

June 7, 1798

CONTENTS

CHAPTER I   1

Question stated – Little prospect of a determination of it,
from the enmity of the opposing parties – The principal
argument against the perfectibility of man and of society
has never been fairly answered – Nature of the difficulty
arising from population – Outline of the principal argument of the essay.

CHAPTER II   7

The different ratios in which population and food increase – The necessary effects of these different ratios of
increase – Oscillation produced by them in the condition
of the lower classes of society – Reasons why this oscillation has not been so much observed as might be expected –
Three propositions on which the general argument of the
essay depends – The different states in which mankind
have been known to exist proposed to be examined with
reference to these three propositions.

CHAPTER III   14

The savage or hunter state shortly reviewed – The shep-
herd state, or the tribes of barbarians that overran the
Roman Empire – The superiority of the power of population to the means of subsistence—the cause of the great
tide of Northern Emigration.

CHAPTER IV   19

State of civilized nations – Probability that Europe is
much more populous now than in the time of Julius
Caesar – Best criterion of population – Probable error of
Hume in one of the criterions that he proposes as assisting
in an estimate of population – Slow increase of population
at present in most of the states of Europe – The two principal checks to population – The first, or preventive check
examined with regard to England.

CHAPTER V   25

The second, or positive check to population examined, in
England – The true cause why the immense sum collected
in England for the poor does not better their condition –
The powerful tendency of the poor laws to defeat their
own purpose – Palliative of the distresses of the poor
proposed – The absolute impossibility from the fixed laws
of our nature, that the pressure of want can ever be completely removed from the lower classes of society – All the
checks to population may be resolved into misery or vice.

CHAPTER VI   36

New colonies – Reasons of their rapid increase – North
American Colonies – Extraordinary instance of increase
in the back settlements – Rapidity with which even old
states recover the ravages of war, pestilence, famine, or the
convulsions of nature.

CHAPTER VII   40

A probable cause of epidemics – Extracts from Mr. Susmilch's tables – Periodical returns of sickly seasons to be
expected in certain cases – Proportion of births to burials
for short periods in any country an inadequate criterion
of the real average increase of population – Best criterion
of a permanent increase of population – Great frugality
of living one of the causes of the famines of China and
Indostan – Evil tendency of one of the clauses in Mr.
Pitt's Poor Bill – Only one proper way of encouraging
population – Causes of the happiness of nations – Famine,
the last and most dreadful mode by which nature represses
a redundant population – The three propositions considered as established.

CHAPTER VIII   50

Mr. Wallace – Error of supposing that the difficulty arising
from population is at a great distance – Mr. Condorcet's
sketch of the progress of the human mind – Period when
the oscillation, mentioned by Mr. Condorcet, ought to be
applied to the human race.

CHAPTER IX   55

Mr. Condorcet's conjecture concerning the organic perfectibility of man, and the indefinite prolongation of

human life – Fallacy of the argument, which infers an
unlimited progress from a partial improvement, the limit
of which cannot be ascertained, illustrated in the breeding
of animals, and the cultivation of plants.

CHAPTER X   61

Mr. Godwin's system of equality – Error of attributing all
the vices of mankind to human institutions – Mr. Godwin's first answer to the difficulty arising from population
totally insufficient – Mr. Godwin's beautiful system of
equality supposed to be realized – Its utter destruction
simply from the principle of population in so short a
time as thirty years.

CHAPTER XI   74

Mr. Godwin's conjecture concerning the future extinction
of the passion between the sexes – Little apparant grounds
for such a conjecture – Passion of love not inconsistent
either with reason or virtue.

CHAPTER XII   77

Mr. Godwin's conjecture concerning the indefinite prolongation of human life – Improper inference drawn from
the effects of mental stimulants on the human frame, illustrated in various instances – Conjectures not founded on
any indications in the past, not to be considered as philosophical conjectures – Mr. Godwin's and Mr. Condorcet's
conjecture respecting the approach of man towards immortality on earth, a curious instance of the inconsistency
of scepticism.

CHAPTER XIII   88

Error of Mr. Godwin in considering man too much in the
light of a being merely rational – In the compound being,
man, the passions will always act as disturbing forces in
the decisions of the understanding – Reasonings of Mr.
Godwin on the subject of coercion – Some truths of a nature not to be communicated from one man to another.

CHAPTER XIV   93

Mr. Godwin's five propositions respecting political truth,
on which his whole work hinges, not established – Reasons
we have for supposing from the distress occasioned by the

principle of population, that the vices, and moral weakness of man can never be wholly eradicated – Perfectibility, in the sense in which Mr. Godwin uses the term, not applicable to man – Nature of the real perfectibility of man illustrated.

CHAPTER XV   98

Models too perfect, may sometimes rather impede than promote improvement – Mr. Godwin's essay on avarice and profusion – Impossibility of dividing the necessary labour of a society amicably among all – Invectives against labour may produce present evil, with little or no chance of producing future good – An accession to the mass of agricultural labour must always be an advantage to the labourer.

CHAPTER XVI   106

Probable error of Dr. Adam Smith in representing every increase of the revenue or stock of a society as an increase in the funds for the maintenance of labour – Instances where an increase of wealth can have no tendency to better the condition of the labouring poor – England has increased in riches without a proportional increase in the funds for the maintenance of labour – The state of the poor in China would not be improved by an increase of wealth from manufactures.

CHAPTER XVII   114

Question of the proper definition of the wealth of a state – Reason given by the French Economists for considering all manufacturers as unproductive labourers, not the true reason – The labour of artificers and manufacturers sufficiently productive to individuals, though not to the state – A remarkable passage in Dr. Price's two volumes of observations – Error of Dr. Price in attributing the happiness and rapid population of America, chiefly, to its peculiar state of civilization – No advantage can be expected from shutting our eyes to the difficulties in the way to the improvement of society.

CHAPTER XVIII   122

The constant pressure of distress on man, from the principle of population, seems to direct our hopes to the

future – State of trial inconsistent with our ideas of the
foreknowledge of God – The world, probably, a mighty
process for awakening matter into mind – Theory of the
formation of mind – Excitements from the wants of the
body – Excitements from the operation of general laws –
Excitements from the difficulties of life arising from the
principle of population.

CHAPTER XIX   131

The sorrows of life necessary to soften and humanize the
heart – The excitements of social sympathy often produce
characters of a higher order than the mere possessors of
talents – Moral evil probably necessary to the production
of moral excellence – Excitements from intellectual wants
continually kept up by the infinite variety of nature, and
the obscurity that involves metaphysical subjects – The
difficulties in Revelation to be accounted for upon this
principle – The degree of evidence which the scriptures
contain, probably, best suited to the improvement of the
human faculties, and the moral amelioration of mankind –
The idea that mind is created by excitements, seems to
account for the existence of natural and moral evil.

CHAPTER I

The great and unlooked for discoveries that have taken place of late years in natural philosophy, the increasing diffusion of general knowledge from the extension of the art of printing, the ardent and unshackled spirit of inquiry that prevails throughout the lettered and even unlettered world, the new and extraordinary lights that have been thrown on political subjects which dazzle and astonish the understanding, and particularly that tremendous phenomenon in the political horizon, the French revolution, which, like a blazing comet, seems destined either to inspire with fresh life and vigour, or to scorch up and destroy the shrinking inhabitants of the earth, have all concurred to lead many able men into the opinion that we were touching on a period big with the most important changes, changes that would in some measure be decisive of the future fate of mankind.

It has been said that the great question is now at issue, whether man shall henceforth start forwards with accelerated velocity towards illimitable, and hitherto unconceived improvement, or be condemned to a perpetual oscillation between happiness and misery, and after every effort remain still at an immeasurable distance from the wished-for goal.

Yet, anxiously as every friend of mankind must look forwards to the termination of this painful suspense, and eagerly as the inquiring mind would hail every ray of light that might assist its view into futurity, it is much to be lamented that the writers on each side of this momentous question still keep far aloof from each other. Their mutual arguments do not meet with a candid examination. The question is not brought to rest on fewer points, and even in theory scarcely seems to be approaching to a decision.

The advocate for the present order of things is apt to treat the sect of speculative philosophers either as a set of artful and designing knaves who preach up ardent benevolence and draw captivating pictures of a happier state of society only the better to enable them to destroy the present establishments and to forward their own deep-laid schemes of ambition, or as wild and mad-headed enthusiasts whose silly speculations and absurd paradoxes are not worthy the attention of any reasonable man.

The advocate for the perfectibility of man, and of society, retorts on the defender of establishments a more than equal contempt. He brands him as the slave of the most miserable and narrow prejudices; or, as the defender of the abuses of civil society, only because he profits by them. He paints him either as a character who prostitutes his understanding to his interest, or as one whose powers of mind are not of a size to grasp any thing great and noble, who cannot see above five yards before him, and who must therefore be utterly unable to take in the views of the enlightened benefactor of mankind.

In this unamicable contest the cause of truth cannot but suffer. The really good arguments on each side of the question are not allowed to have their proper weight. Each pursues his own theory, little solicitous to correct or improve it by an attention to what is advanced by his opponents.

The friend of the present order of things condemns all political speculations in the gross. He will not even condescend to examine the grounds from which the perfectibility of society is inferred. Much less will he give himself the trouble in a fair and candid manner to attempt an exposition of their fallacy.

The speculative philosopher equally offends against the cause of truth. With eyes fixed on a happier state of society, the blessings of which he paints in the most captivating colours, he allows himself to indulge in the most bitter invectives against every present establishment, without applying his talents to consider the best and safest means of removing abuses and without seeming to be aware of the tremendous obstacles that threaten, even in theory, to oppose the progress of man towards perfection.

It is an acknowledged truth in philosophy that a just theory will always be confirmed by experiment. Yet so much friction, and so many minute circumstances occur in practice, which it is next to impossible for the most enlarged and penetrating mind to foresee, that on few subjects can any theory be pronounced just, that has not stood the test of experience. But an untried theory cannot fairly be advanced as probable, much less as just, till all the arguments against it have been maturely weighed and clearly and consistently refuted.

I have read some of the speculations on the perfectibility of man and of society with great pleasure. I have been warmed and delighted with the enchanting picture which they hold forth. I ardently wish for such happy improvements. But I see great, and, to my understanding, unconquerable difficulties in the way to them. These difficulties it is my present purpose to state, declaring, at the same time, that so far from exulting in them, as a cause of triumph over the friends of innovation, nothing would give me greater pleasure than to see them completely removed.

The most important argument that I shall adduce is certainly not new. The principles on which it depends have been explained in part by Hume, and more at large by Dr. Adam Smith. It has been advanced and applied to the present subject, though not with its proper weight, or in the most forcible point of view, by Mr. Wallace, and it may probably have been stated by many writers that I have never met with. I should certainly therefore not think of advancing it again, though I mean to place it in a point of view in some degree different from any that I have hitherto seen, if it had ever been fairly and satisfactorily answered.

The cause of this neglect on the part of the advocates for the perfectibility of mankind is not easily accounted for. I cannot doubt the talents of such men as Godwin and Condorcet. I am unwilling to doubt their candour. To my understanding, and probably to that of most others, the difficulty appears insurmountable. Yet these men of acknowledged ability and penetration, scarcely deign to notice it, and hold on their course in such speculations, with unabated ardour and undiminished confidence. I have certainly no right to say that they purposely shut their eyes to such arguments. I ought rather to doubt the validity of them, when neglected by such men, however forcibly their truth may strike my own mind. Yet in this respect it must be acknowledged that we are all of us too prone to err. If I saw a glass of wine repeatedly presented to a man, and he took no notice of it, I should be apt to think that he was blind or uncivil. A juster philosophy might teach me rather to think that my eyes deceived me and that the offer was not really what I conceived it to be.

In entering upon the argument I must premise that I put out of the question, at present, all mere conjectures, that is, all suppositions, the probable realization of which cannot be inferred upon any just philosophical grounds. A writer may tell me that he thinks man will ultimately become an ostrich. I cannot properly contradict him. But before he can expect to bring any reasonable person over to his opinion, he ought to shew, that the necks of mankind have been gradually elongating, that the lips have grown harder and more prominent, that the legs and feet are daily altering their shape, and that the hair is beginning to change into stubs of feathers. And till the probability of so wonderful a conversion can be shewn, it is surely lost time and lost eloquence to expatiate on the happiness of man in such a state; to describe his powers, both of running and flying, to paint him in a condition where all narrow luxuries would be contemned, where he would be employed only in collecting the necessaries of life, and where, consequently, each man's share of labour would be light, and his portion of leisure ample.

I think I may fairly make two postulata.

First, That food is necessary to the existence of man.

Secondly, That the passion between the sexes is necessary and will remain nearly in its present state.

These two laws, ever since we have had any knowledge of mankind, appear to have been fixed laws of our nature, and, as we have not hitherto seen any alteration in them, we have no right to conclude that they will ever cease to be what they now are, without an immediate act of power in that Being who first arranged the system of the universe, and for the advantage of his creatures, still executes, according to fixed laws, all its various operations.

I do not know that any writer has supposed that on this earth man will ultimately be able to live without food. But Mr. Godwin has conjectured that the passion between the sexes may in time be extinguished. As, however, he calls this part of his work a deviation into the land of conjecture, I will not dwell longer upon it at present than to say that the best arguments for the perfectibility of man are drawn from a contemplation of the great progress that he has already made from the savage state and the difficulty of saying where he is to stop. But towards the extinction of the passion between the sexes, no progress whatever has hitherto been made. It appears to exist in as much force at present as it did two thousand or four thousand years ago. There are individual exceptions now as there always have been. But, as these exceptions do not appear to increase in number, it would surely be a very unphilosophical mode of arguing, to infer merely from the existence of an exception, that the exception would, in time, become the rule, and the rule the exception.

Assuming then, my postulata as granted, I say, that the power of population is indefinitely greater than the power in the earth to produce subsistence for man.

Population, when unchecked, increases in a geometrical ratio. Subsistence increases only in an arithmetical ratio. A slight acquaintance with numbers will shew the immensity of the first power in comparison of the second.

By that law of our nature which makes food necessary to the life of man, the effects of these two unequal powers must be kept equal.

This implies a strong and constantly operating check on population from the difficulty of subsistence. This difficulty must fall some where and must necessarily be severely felt by a large portion of mankind.

Through the animal and vegetable kingdoms, nature has scattered the seeds of life abroad with the most profuse and liberal hand. She has been comparatively sparing in the room and the nourishment necessary to rear them. The germs of existence contained in this spot of earth, with ample food, and ample room to expand in, would fill millions of worlds in the course of a few thousand years. Necessity, that imperious all pervading law of nature, restrains them within the prescribed bounds. The race of plants, and the race of animals shrink under this great restrictive law. And the race of man cannot, by any efforts of reason, escape from it. Among plants and animals its effects are waste of seed, sickness, and premature death. Among mankind, misery and vice. The former, misery, is an absolutely necessary consequence of it. Vice is a highly probable consequence, and we therefore see it abundantly prevail, but it ought not, perhaps, to be called an absolutely necessary consequence. The ordeal of virtue is to resist all temptation to evil.

This natural inequality of the two powers of population and of production in the earth and that great law of our nature which must constantly keep their effects equal form the great difficulty that to me appears insurmountable in the way to the perfectibility of society. All other arguments are of slight and subordinate consideration in comparison of this. I see no way by which man can escape from the weight of this law which pervades all animated nature. No fancied equality, no agrarian regulations in their utmost extent, could remove the pressure of it even for a single century. And it appears, therefore, to be decisive against the possible existence of a society, all the members of which should live in ease, happiness, and comparative leisure; and feel no anxiety about providing the means of subsistence for themselves and families.

Consequently, if the premises are just, the argument is conclusive against the perfectibility of the mass of mankind.

I have thus sketched the general outline of the argument, but I will examine it more particularly, and I think it will be found that experience, the true source and foundation of all knowledge, invariably confirms its truth.

CHAPTER II

I said that population, when unchecked, increased in a geometrical ratio, and subsistence for man in an arithmetical ratio.

Let us examine whether this position be just.

I think it will be allowed, that no state has hitherto existed (at least that we have any account of) where the manners were so pure and simple, and the means of subsistence so abundant, that no check whatever has existed to early marriages, among the lower classes, from a fear of not providing well for their families, or among the higher classes, from a fear of lowering their condition in life. Consequently in no state that we have yet known has the power of population been left to exert itself with perfect freedom.

Whether the law of marriage be instituted or not, the dictate of nature and virtue seems to be an early attachment to one woman. Supposing a liberty of changing in the case of an unfortunate choice, this liberty would not affect population till it arose to a height greatly vicious; and we are now supposing the existence of a society where vice is scarcely known.

In a state therefore of great equality and virtue, where pure and simple manners prevailed, and where the means of subsistence were so abundant that no part of the society could have any fears about providing amply for a family, the power of population being left to exert itself unchecked, the increase of the human species would evidently be much greater than any increase that has been hitherto known.

In the United States of America, where the means of subsistence have been more ample, the manners of the people more pure, and consequently the checks to early marriages fewer than in any of the modern states of Europe, the population has been found to double itself in twenty-five years.

This ratio of increase, though short of the utmost power of population, yet as the result of actual experience, we will take as our rule, and say, that population, when unchecked, goes on doubling itself every twenty-five years or increases in a geometrical ratio.

Let us now take any spot of earth, this Island for instance, and see in what ratio the subsistence it affords can be supposed to increase. We will begin with it under its present state of cultivation.

If I allow that by the best possible policy, by breaking up more land and by great encouragements to agriculture, the produce of this Island may be doubled in the first twenty-five years, I think it will be allowing as much as any person can well demand.

In the next twenty-five years, it is impossible to suppose that the produce could be quadrupled. It would be contrary to all our knowledge of the qualities of land. The very utmost that we can conceive, is, that the increase in the second twenty-five years might equal the present produce. Let us then take this for our rule, though certainly far beyond the truth, and allow that by great exertion, the whole produce of the Island might be increased every twenty-five years, by a quantity of subsistence equal to what it at present produces. The most enthusiastic speculator cannot suppose a greater increase than this. In a few centuries it would make every acre of land in the Island like a garden.

Yet this ratio of increase is evidently arithmetical.

It may be fairly said, therefore, that the means of subsistence increase in an arithmetical ratio. Let us now bring the effects of these two ratios together.

The population of the Island is computed to be about seven millions, and we will suppose the present produce equal to the support of such a number. In the first twenty-five years the population would be fourteen millions, and the food being also doubled, the means of subsistence would be equal to this increase. In the next twenty-five years the population would be twenty-eight millions, and the means of subsistence only equal to the support of twenty-one millions. In the next period, the population would be fifty-six millions, and the means of subsistence just sufficient

THE FIRST ESSAY
9

for half that number. And at the conclusion of the first century the population would be one hundred and twelve millions and the means of subsistence only equal to the support of thirty-five millions, which would leave a population of seventy-seven millions totally unprovided for.

A great emigration necessarily implies unhappiness of some kind or other in the country that is deserted. For few persons will leave their families, connections, friends, and native land, to seek á settlement in untried foreign climes, without some strong subsisting causes of uneasiness where they are, or the hope of some great advantages in the place to which they are going.

But to make the argument more general and less interrupted by the partial views of emigration, let us take the whole earth, instead of one spot, and suppose that the restraints to population were universally removed. If the subsistence for man that the earth affords was to be increased every twenty-five years by a quantity equal to what the whole world at present produces, this would allow the power of production in the earth to be absolutely unlimited, and its ratio of increase much greater than we can conceive that any possible exertions of mankind could make it.

Taking the population of the world at any number, a thousand millions, for instance, the human species would increase in the ratio of—1, 2, 4, 8, 16, 32, 64, 128, 256, 512, &c. and subsistence as—1, 2, 3, 4, 5, 6, 7, 8, 9, 10, &c. In two centuries and a quarter, the population would be to the means of subsistence as 512 to 10: in three centuries as 4096 to 13, and in two thousand years the difference would be almost incalculable, though the produce in that time would have increased to an immense extent.

No limits whatever are placed to the productions of the earth; they may increase for ever and be greater than any assignable quantity; yet still the power of population being a power of a superior order, the increase of the human species can only be kept commensurate to the increase of the means of subsistence, by the constant operation of the strong law of necessity acting as a check upon the greater power.

The effects of this check remain now to be considered.

Among plants and animals the view of the subject is simple. They are all impelled by a powerful instinct to the increase of their species, and this instinct is interrupted by no reasoning or doubts about providing for their offspring. Wherever therefore there is liberty, the power of increase is exerted, and the super-abundant effects are repressed afterwards by want of room and nourishment, which is common to animals and plants, and among animals, by becoming the prey of others.

The effects of this check on man are more complicated. Impelled to the increase of his species by an equally powerful instinct, reason interrupts his career and asks him whether he may not bring beings into the world, for whom he cannot provide the means of subsistence. In a state of equality, this would be the simple question. In the present state of society, other considerations occur. Will he not lower his rank in life? Will he not subject himself to greater difficulties than he at present feels? Will he not be obliged to labour harder? and if he has a large family, will his utmost exertions enable him to support them? May he not see his offspring in rags and misery, and clamouring for bread that he cannot give them? And may he not be reduced to the grating necessity of forfeiting his independence, and of being obliged to the sparing hand of charity for support?

These considerations are calculated to prevent, and certainly do prevent, a very great number in all civilized nations from pursuing the dictate of nature in an early attachment to one woman. And this restraint almost necessarily, though not absolutely so, pro-duces vice. Yet in all societies, even those that are most vicious, the tendency to a virtuous attachment is so strong that there is a constant effort towards an increase of population. This constant effort as constantly tends to subject the lower classes of the society to distress and to prevent any great permanent amelioration of their condition.

The way in which these effects are produced seems to be this.

We will suppose the means of subsistence in any country just equal to the easy support of its inhabitants. The constant effort towards population, which is found to act even in the most vicious societies, increases the number of people before the means of subsistence are increased. The food therefore which before sup-ported seven millions must now be divided among seven millions and a half or eight millions. The poor consequently must live much worse, and many of them be reduced to severe distress. The number of labourers also being above the proportion of the work in the market, the price of labour must tend toward a decrease, while the price of provisions would at the same time tend to rise. The labourer therefore must work harder to earn the same as he did before. During this season of distress, the discouragements to marriage, and the difficulty of rearing a family are so great that population is at a stand. In the mean time the cheapness of labour, the plenty of labourers, and the necessity of an increased industry amongst them, encourage cultivators to employ more labour upon their land, to turn up fresh soil, and to manure and improve more completely what is already in tillage, till ultimately the means of subsistence become in the same proportion to the population as at the period from which we set out. The situation of the labourer being then again tolerably comfortable, the restraints to population are in some degree loosened, and the same retrograde and progressive movements with respect to happiness are repeated.

This sort of oscillation will not be remarked by superficial observers, and it may be difficult even for the most penetrating mind to calculate its periods. Yet that in all old states some such vibration does exist, though from various transverse causes, in a much less marked, and in a much more irregular manner than I have described it, no reflecting man who considers the subject deeply can well doubt.

Many reasons occur why this oscillation has been less obvious, and less decidedly confirmed by experience, than might naturally be expected.

One principal reason is that the histories of mankind that we possess are histories only of the higher classes. We have but few accounts that can be depended upon of the manners and customs of that part of mankind, where these retrograde and progressive movements chiefly take place. A satisfactory history of this kind, of one people, and of one period, would require the constant and minute attention of an observing mind during a long life. Some of the objects of enquiry would be, in what proportion to the number of adults was the number of marriages, to what extent vicious customs prevailed in consequence of the restraints upon matrimony, what was the comparative mortality among the children of the most distressed part of the community and those who lived rather more at their ease, what were the variations in the real price of labour, and what were the observable differences in the state of the lower classes of society with respect to ease and happiness, at different times during a certain period.

Such a history would tend greatly to elucidate the manner in which the constant check upon population acts and would probably prove the existence of the retrograde and progressive movements that have been mentioned, though the times of their vibration must necessarily be rendered irregular, from the operation of many interrupting causes, such as the introduction or failure of certain manufactures, a greater or less prevalent spirit of agricultural enterprize, years of plenty, or years of scarcity, wars and pestilence, poor laws, the invention of processes for shortening labour without the proportional extension of the market for the commodity, and, particularly, the difference between the nominal and real price of labour, a circumstance which has perhaps more than any other contributed to conceal this oscillation from common view.

It very rarely happens that the nominal price of labour universally falls, but we well know that it frequently remains the same, while the nominal price of provisions has been gradually increasing. This is, in effect, a real fall in the price of labour, and during this period the condition of the lower orders of the community must gradually grow worse and worse. But the farmers and capitalists are growing rich from the real cheapness of labour. Their increased capitals enable them to employ a greater number of men. Work therefore may be plentiful, and the price of labour would consequently rise. But the want of freedom in the market of labour, which occurs more or less in all communities, either from parish laws, or the more general cause of the facility of combination among the rich, and its difficulty among the poor, operates to prevent the price of labour from rising at the natural period, and keeps it down some time longer; perhaps, till a year of scarcity, when the clamour is too loud, and the necessity too apparent to be resisted.

The true cause of the advance in the price of labour is thus concealed, and the rich affect to grant it as an act of compassion and favour to the poor, in consideration of a year of scarcity, and, when plenty returns, indulge themselves in the most unreasonable of all complaints, that the price does not again fall, when a little reflection would shew them that it must have risen long before but from an unjust conspiracy of their own.

But though the rich by unfair combinations contribute frequently to prolong a season of distress among the poor, yet no possible form of society could prevent the almost constant action of misery upon a great part of mankind, if in a state of inequality, and upon all, if all were equal.

The theory on which the truth of this position depends appears to me so extremely clear that I feel at a loss to conjecture what part of it can be denied.

That population cannot increase without the means of subsistence is a proposition so evident that it needs no illustration.

That population does invariably increase where there are the means of subsistence, the history of every people that have ever existed will abundantly prove.

And that the superior power of population cannot be checked without producing misery or vice, the ample portion of these too bitter ingredients in the cup of human life and the continuance of the physical causes that seem to have produced them bear too convincing a testimony.

But in order more fully to ascertain the validity of these three propositions, let us examine the different states in which mankind have been known to exist. Even a cursory review will, I think, be sufficient to convince us that these propositions are incontrovertible truths.

CHAPTER III

In the rudest state of mankind, in which hunting is the principal occupation, and the only mode of acquiring food, the means of subsistence being scattered over a large extent of territory, the comparative population must necessarily be thin. It is said that the passion between the sexes is less ardent among the North American Indians than among any other race of men. Yet notwithstanding this apathy, the effort towards population, even in this people, seems to be always greater than the means to support it. This appears from the comparatively rapid population that takes place whenever any of the tribes happen to settle in some fertile spot and to draw nourishment from more fruitful sources than that of hunting, and it has been frequently remarked that when an Indian family has taken up its abode near any European settlement and adopted a more easy and civilized mode of life, that one woman has reared five or six, or more children, though in the savage state it rarely happens, that above one or two in a family grow up to maturity. The same observation has been made with regard to the Hottentots near the Cape. These facts prove the superior power of population to the means of subsistence in nations of hunters, and that this power always shews itself the moment it is left to act with freedom.

It remains to inquire whether this power can be checked, and its effects kept equal to the means of subsistence, without vice or misery.

The North American Indians, considered as a people, cannot justly be called free and equal. In all the accounts we have of them, and, indeed, of most other savage nations, the women are represented as much more completely in a state of slavery to the

men than the poor are to the rich in civilized countries. One half
the nation appears to act as Helots to the other half, and the
misery that checks population falls chiefly, as it always must do,
upon that part whose condition is lowest in the scale of society.
The infancy of man in the simplest state requires considerable
attention, but this necessary attention the women cannot give,
condemned as they are to the inconveniences and hardships of
frequent change of place and to the constant and unremitting
drudgery of preparing every thing for the reception of their
tyrannic lords. These exertions, sometimes during pregnancy or
with children at their backs, must occasion frequent miscarriages,
and prevent any but the most robust infants from growing to
maturity. Add to these hardships of the women, the constant war
that prevails among savages, and the necessity which they frequently labour under of exposing their aged and helpless parents,
and of thus violating the first feelings of nature, and the picture
will not appear very free from the blot of misery. In estimating the
happiness of a savage nation, we must not fix our eyes only on the
warrior in the prime of life: he is one of a hundred: he is the
gentleman, the man of fortune, the chances have been in his
favour; and many efforts have failed ere this fortunate being was
produced, whose guardian genius should preserve him through
the numberless dangers with which he would be surrounded from
infancy to manhood. The true points of comparison between two
nations, seem to be, the ranks in each which appear nearest to
answer to each other. And in this view, I should compare the
warriors in the prime of life with the gentlemen, and the women,
children, and aged, with the lower classes of the community in
civilized states.

May we not then fairly infer from this short review, or rather,
from the accounts that may be referred to of nation of hunters,
that their population is thin from the scarcity of food, that it
would immediately increase if food was in greater plenty, and
that, putting vice out of the question among savages, misery is
the check that represses the superior power of population and
keeps its effects equal to the means of subsistence. Actual observation and experience tell us that this check, with a few local and
temporary exceptions is constantly acting now upon all savage

nations, and the theory indicates, that it probably acted with nearly equal strength a thousand years ago, and it may not be much greater a thousand years hence.

Of the manners and habits that prevail among nations of shepherds, the next state of mankind, we are even more ignorant than of the savage state. But that these nations could not escape the general lot of misery arising from the want of subsistence, Europe, and all the fairest countries in the world, bear ample testimony. Want was the goad that drove the Scythian shepherds from their native haunts, like so many famished wolves in search of prey. Set in motion by this all powerful cause, clouds of Barbarians seemed to collect from all points of the northern hemisphere. Gathering fresh darkness and terror as they rolled on, the congregated bodies at length obscured the sun of Italy and sunk the whole world in universal night. These tremendous effects, so long and so deeply felt throughout the fairest portions of the earth, may be traced to the simple cause of the superior power of population, to the means of subsistence.

It is well known that a country in pasture cannot support so many inhabitants as a country in tillage, but what renders nations of shepherds so formidable is the power which they possess of moving all togeter and the necessity they frequently feel of exerting this power in search of fresh pasture for their herds. A tribe that was rich in cattle had an immediate plenty of food. Even the parent stock might be devoured in a case of absolute necessity. The women lived in greater ease than among nations of hunters. The men bold in their united strength and confiding in their power of procuring pasture for their cattle by change of place, felt, probably, but few fears about providing for a family. These combined causes soon produced their natural and invariable effect on extended population. A more frequent and rapid change of place became then necessary. A wider and more extensive territory was successively occupied. A broader desolation extended all around them. Want pinched the less fortunate members of the society, and, at length, the impossibility of supporting such a number together became too evident to be resisted. Young scions were then pushed out from the parent-stock and instructed to explore fresh regions and to gain happier seats for themselves by their swords. "The world was all before them where to chuse." Restless from present distress, flushed with the hope of fairer prospects, and animated with the spirit of hardy enterprize, these daring adventurers were likely to become formidable adversaries to all who opposed them. The peaceful inhabitants of the countries on which they rushed could not long withstand the energy of men acting under such powerful motives of exertion. And when they fell in with any tribes like their own, the contest was a struggle for existence, and they fought with a desperate courage, inspired by the reflection that death was the punishment of defeat and life the prize of victory.

In these savage contests many tribes must have been utterly exterminated. Some, probably, perished by hardship and famine. Others, whose leading star had given them a happier direction, became great and powerful tribes, and, in their turns, sent off fresh adventurers in search of still more fertile seats. The prodigious waste of human life occasioned by this perpetual struggle for room and food was more than supplied by the mighty power of population, acting, in some degree, unshackled from the constant habit of emigration. The tribes that migrated towards the South, though they won these more fruitful regions by continual battles, rapidly increased in number and power, from the increased means of subsistence. Till at length, the whole territory, from the confines of China to the shores of the Baltic was peopled by a various race of Barbarians, brave, robust, and enterprising, inured to hardship, and delighting in war. Some tribes maintained their independence. Others ranged themselves under the standard of some barbaric chieftain who led them to victory after victory, and what was of more importance, to regions abounding in corn, wine, and oil, the long wished for consummation, and great reward of their labours. An Alaric, an Attila, or a Zingis Khan, and the chiefs around them, might fight for glory, for the fame of extensive conquests, but the true cause that set in motion the great tide of northern emigration, and that continued to propel it till it rolled at different periods, against China, Persia, Italy, and even Egypt, was a scarcity of food, a population extended beyond the means of supporting it.

The absolute population at any one period, in proportion to

the extent of territory, could never be great, on account of the unproductive nature of some of the regions occupied; but there appears to have been a most rapid succession of human beings, and as fast as some were mowed down by the scythe of war or of famine, others rose in increased numbers to supply their place. Among these bold and improvident Barbarians, population was probably but little checked, as in modern states, from a fear of future difficulties. A prevailing hope of bettering their condition by change of place, a constant expectation of plunder, a power even, if distressed, of selling their children as slaves, added to the natural carelessness of the barbaric character, all conspired to raise a population which remained to be repressed afterwards by famine or war.

Were there is any inequality of conditions, and among nations of shepherds this soon takes place, the distress arising from a scarcity of provisions, must fall hardest upon the least fortunate members of the society. This distress also must frequently have been felt by the women, exposed to casual plunder in the absence of their husbands, and subject to continual disappointments in their expected return.

But without knowing enough of the minute and intimate history of these people, to point out precisely on what part the distress for want of food chiefly fell, and to what extent it was generally felt, I think we may fairly say, from all the accounts that we have of nations of shepherds, that population invariably increased among them whenever, by emigration or any other cause, the means of subsistence were increased, and that a further population was checked, and the actual population kept equal to the means of subsistence by misery and vice.

For, independently of any vicious customs that might have prevailed amongst them with regard to women, which always operate as checks to population, it must be acknowledged I think, that the commission of war is vice, and the effect of it misery, and none can doubt the misery of want of food.

CHAPTER IV

In examining the next state of mankind with relation to the question before us, the state of mixed pasture and tillage, in which with some variation in the proportions the most civilized nations must always remain, we shall be assisted in our review by what we daily see around us, by actual experience, by facts that come within the scope of every man's observation.

Notwithstanding the exaggerations of some old historians, there can remain no doubt in the mind of any thinking man that the population of the principal countries of Europe, France, England, Germany, Russia, Poland, Sweden, and Denmark is much greater than ever it was in former times. The obvious reason of these exaggerations is the formidable aspect that even a thinly peopled nation must have, when collected together and moving all at once in search of fresh seats. If to this tremendous appearance be added a succession at certain intervals of similar emigrations, we shall not be much surprised that the fears of the timid nations of the South, represented the North as a region absolutely swarming with human beings. A nearer and juster view of the subject at present enables us to see that the inference was as absurd as if a man in this country, who was continually meeting on the road drove of cattle from Wales ad the North, was immediately to conclude that these countries were the most productive of all the parts of the kingdom.

The reason that the greater part of Europe is more populous now than it was in former times, is that the industry of the inhabitants has made these countries produce a greater quantity of human subsistence. For, I conceive, that it may be laid down as a position not to be controverted, that, taking a sufficient extent of territory to include within it exportation and importation, and

allowing some variation for the prevalence of luxury, or of frugal
habits, that population constantly bears a regular proportion to
the food that the earth is made to produce. In the controversy
concerning the populousness of ancient and modern nations, could
it be clearly ascertained that the average produce of the countries
in question, taken altogether, is greater now than it was in the
times of Julius Caesar, the dispute would be at once determined.

When we are assured that China is the most fertile country in the
world, that almost all the land is in tillage, and that a great part
of it bears two crops every year, and further, that the people live
very frugally, we may infer with certainty, that the population
must be immense, without busying ourselves in inquiries into the
manners and habits of the lower classes and the encouragements to
early marriages. But these inquiries are of the utmost importance,
and a minute history of the customs of the lower Chinese would
be of the greatest use in ascertaining in what manner the checks
to a further population operate; what are the vices, and what are
the distresses that prevent an increase of numbers beyond the
ability of the country to support.

Hume, in his essay on the populousness of ancient and modern
nations, when he intermingles, as he says, an inquiry concerning
causes with that concerning facts, does not seem to see with his
usual penetration how very little some of the causes he alludes to
could enable him to form any judgment of the actual population
of ancient nations. If any inference can be drawn from them,
perhaps it should be directly the reverse of what Hume draws,
though I certainly ought to speak with great diffidence in dis-
senting from a man, who of all others on such subjects was the
least likely to be deceived by first appearances. If I find that at a
certain period in ancient history, the encouragements to have a
family were great, that early marriages were consequently very
prevalent, and that few persons remained single, I should infer
with certainty that population was rapidly increasing, but by no
means that it was then actually very great, rather, indeed, the
contrary, that it was then thin and that there was room and food
for a much greater number. On the other hand, if I find that at
this period the difficulties attending a family were very great,
that, consequently, few early marriages took place, and that a great

number of both sexes remained single, I infer with certainty that population was at a stand, and, probably, because the actual population was very great in proportion to the fertility of the land and that there was scarcely room and food for more. The number of footmen, housemaids, and other persons remaining unmarried in modern states, Hume allows to be rather an argument against their population. I should rather draw a contrary inference and consider it an argument of their fullness, though this inference is not certain, because there are many thinly inhabited states that are yet stationary in their population. To speak, therefore, correctly, perhaps it may be said that the number of unmarried persons in proportion to the whole number, existing at different periods, in the same or different states will enable us to judge whether population at these periods was increasing, stationary, or decreasing, but will form no criterion by which we can determine the actual population.

There is, however, a circumstance taken notice of in most of the accounts we have of China that it seems difficult to reconcile with this reasoning. It is said that early marriages very generally prevail through all the ranks of the Chinese. Yet Dr. Adam Smith supposes that population in China is stationary. These two circumstances appear to be irreconcileable. It certainly seems very little probable that the population of China is fast increasing. Every acre of land has been so long in cultivation that we can hardly conceive there is any great yearly addition to the average produce. The fact, perhaps, of the universality of early marriages may not be sufficiently ascertained. If it be supposed true, the only way of accounting for the difficulty, with our present knowledge of the subject, appears to be that the redundant population, necessarily occasioned by the prevalence of early marriages, must be repressed by occasional famines, and by the custom of exposing children, which, in times of distress, is probably more frequent than is ever acknowledged to Europeans. Relative to this barbarous practice, it is difficult to avoid remarking, that there cannot be a stronger proof of the distresses that have been felt by mankind for want of food, than the existence of a custom that thus violates the most natural principle of the human heart. It appears to have been very general among ancient nations, and certainly tended rather to increase population.

In examining the principal states of modern Europe, we shall find that though they have increased very considerably in population since they were nations of shepherds, yet that at present, their progress is but slow, and instead of doubling their numbers every twenty-five years they require three or four hundred years, or more for that purpose. Some, indeed, may be absolutely stationary, and others even retrograde. The cause of this slow progress in population cannot be traced to a decay of the passion between the sexes. We have sufficient reason to think that this natural propensity exists still in undiminished vigour. Why then do not its effects appear in a rapid increase of the human species? An intimate view of the state of society in any one country in Europe, which may serve equally for all, will enable us to answer this question, and to say that a foresight of the difficulties attending the rearing of a family acts as a preventive check, and the actual distresses of some of the lower classes, by which they are disabled from giving the proper food and attention to their children, acts as a positive check to the natural increase of population.

England, as one of the most flourishing states of Europe, may be fairly taken for an example, and the observations made will apply with but little variation to any other country where the population increases slowly.

The preventive check appears to operate in some degree through all the ranks of society in England. There are some men, even in the highest rank, who are prevented from marrying by the idea of the expenses that they must retrench, and the fancied pleasures that they must deprive themselves of, on the supposition of having a family. These considerations are certainly trivial, but a preventive foresight of this kind has objects of much greater weight for its contemplation as we go lower.

A man of liberal education, but with an income only just sufficient to enable him to associate in the rank of gentlemen, must feel absolutely certain that if he marries and has a family he shall be obliged, if he mixes at all in society, to rank himself with moderate farmers and the lower class of tradesmen. The woman that a man of education would naturally make the object of his choice would be one brought up in the same tastes and sentiments with himself and used to the familiar intercourse of a society totally different from that to which she must be reduced by marriage. Can a man consent to place the object of his affection in a situation so discordant, probably, to her tastes and inclinations? Two or three steps of descent in society, particularly at this round of the ladder, where education ends and ignorance begins, will not be considered by the generality of people as a fancied and chimerical, but a real and essential evil. If society be held desireable, it surely must be free, equal, and reciprocal society, where benefits are conferred as well as received, and not such as the dependent finds with his patron or the poor with the rich.

These considerations undoubtedly prevent a great number in this rank of life from following the bent of their inclinations in an early attachment. Others, guided either by a stronger passion, or a weaker judgment, break through these restraints, and it would be hard indeed, if the gratification of so delightful a passion as virtuous love, did not, sometimes, more than counterbalance all its attendant evils. But I fear It must be owned, that the more general consequences of such marriages, are rather calculated to justify than to repress the forebodings of the prudent.

The sons of tradesmen and farmers are exhorted not to marry, and generally find it necessary to pursue this advice till they are settled in some business, or farm that may enable them to support a family. These events may not, perhaps, occur till they are far advanced in life. The scarcity of farms is a very general complaint in England. And the competition in every kind of business is so great that it is not possible that all should be successful.

The labourer who earns eighteen pence a day and lives with some degree of comfort as a single man, will hesitate a little before he divides that pittance among four or five, which seems to be but just sufficient for one. Harder fare and harder labour he would submit to for the sake of living with the woman that he loves, but he must feel conscious, if he thinks at all, that should he have a large family, and any ill luck whatever, no degree of frugality, no possible exertion of his manual strength could preserve him from the heart rending sensation of seeing his children starve, or of forfeiting his independence, and being obliged to the parish for their support. The love of independence is a sentiment that surely none would wish to be erased from the breast of man, though the parish law of England, it must be confessed, is a system of all others the most calculated gradually to weaken this sentiment, and in the end, may eradicate it completely.

The servants who live in gentlemen's families, have restraints that are yet stronger to break through in venturing upon marriage They possess the necessaries, and even the comforts of life, almost in as great plenty as their masters. Their work is easy and their food luxurious compared with the class of labourers. And their sense of dependence is weakened by the conscious power of changing their masters, if they feel themselves offended. Thus comfortably situated at present, what are their prospects in marrying? Without knowledge or capital, either for business, or farming, and unused, and therefore unable to earn a subsistence by daily labour, their only refuge seems to be a miserable alehouse, which certainly offers no very enchanting prospect of a happy evening to their lives. By much the greater part, therefore, deterred by this uninviting view of their future situation, content themselves with remaining single where they are.

If this sketch of the state of society in England be near the truth, and I do not conceive that it is exaggerated, it will be allowed, that the preventive check to population in this country operates, though with varied force, through all the classes of the community. The same observation will hold true with regard to all old states. The effects, indeed, of these restraints upon marriage are but too conspicuous in the consequent vices that are produced in almost every part of the world, vices, that are continually involving both sexes in inextricable unhappiness.

CHAPTER V

The positive check to population by which I mean the check that represses an increase which is already begun, is confined chiefly, though not perhaps solely, to the lowest orders of society. This check is not so obvious to common view as the other I have mentioned, and, to prove distinctly the force and extent of its operation would require, perhaps, more data than we are in possession of. But I believe it has been very generally remarked by those who have attended to bills of mortality that of the number of children who die annually, much too great a proportion belongs to those who may be supposed unable to give their offspring proper food and attention, exposed as they are occasionally to severe distress and confined, perhaps, to unwholesome habitations and hard labour. This mortality among the children of the poor has been constantly taken notice of in all towns. It certainly does not prevail in an equal degree in the country, but the subject has not hitherto received sufficient attention to enable any one to say that there are not more deaths in proportion among the children of the poor, even in the country, than among those of the middling and higher classes. Indeed, it seems difficult to suppose that a labourer's wife who has six children, and who is sometimes in absolute want of bread, should be able always to give them the food and attention necessary to support life. The sons and daughters of peasants will not be found such rosy cherubs in real life as they are described to be in romances. It cannot fail to be remarked by those who live much in the country that the sons of labourers are very apt to be stunted in their growth, and are a long while arriving at maturity. Boys that you would guess to be fourteen or fifteen, are upon inquiry, frequently found to be eighteen or nineteen. And the lads who drive plough, which must certainly be a healthy exercise, are very rarely seen with any appearance of calves to their legs; a circumstance, which can only be attributed to a want either of proper or of sufficient nourishment.

To remedy the frequent distresses of the common people, the poor laws of England have been instituted; but it is to be feared, that though they may have alleviated a little the intensity of individual misfortune, they have spread the general evil over a much larger surface. It is a subject often started in conversation and mentioned always as a matter of great surprise that notwithstanding the immense sum that is annually collected for the poor in England, there is still so much distress among them. Some think that the money must be embezzled, others that the church-wardens and overseers consume the greater part of it in dinners. All agree that some how or other it must be very ill-managed. In short the fact that nearly three millions are collected annually for the poor and yet that their distresses are not removed is the subject of continual astonishment. But a man who sees a little below the surface of things would be very much more astonished if the fact were otherwise than it is observed to be, or even if a collection universally of eighteen shillings in the pound instead of four, were materially to alter it. I will state a case which I hope will elucidate my meaning.

Suppose, that by a subscription of the rich, the eighteen pence a day which men earn now was made up five shillings, it might be imagined, perhaps, that they would then be able to live comfortably and have a piece of meat every day for their dinners. But this would be a very false conclusion. The transfer of three shillings and sixpence a day to every labourer would not increase the quantity of meat in the country. There is not at present enough for all to have a decent share. What would then be the consequence? The competition among the buyers in the market of meat would rapidly raise the price from six pence or seven pence, to two or three shillings in the pound, and the commodity would not be divided among many more than it is at present. When an article is scarce, and cannot be distributed to all, he that can shew the most valid patent, that is, he that offers most money becomes the possessor. If we can suppose the competition among the buyers of meat to continue long enough for a greater number of cattle to be reared annually, this could only be done at the expense of the corn, which would be a very disadvantageous exchange, for it is well known that the country could not then support the same population, and when subsistence is scarce in proportion to the number of people, it is of little consequence whether the lowest members of the society possess eighteen pence or five shillings. They must at all events be reduced to live upon the hardest fare and in the smallest quantity.

It will be said, perhaps, that the increased number of purchasers in every article would give a spur to productive industry and that the whole produce of the island would be increased. This might in some degree be the case. But the spur that these fancied riches would give to population would more than counterbalance it, and the increased produce would be to be divided among a more than proportionably increased number of people. All this time I am supposing that the same quantity of work would be done as before. But this would not really take place. The receipt of five shillings a day, instead of eighteen pence, would make every man fancy himself comparatively rich and able to indulge himself in many hours or days of leisure. This would give a strong and immediate check to productive industry, and in a short time, not only the nation would be poorer, but the lower classes themselves would be much more distressed than when they received only eighteen pence a day.

A collection from the rich of eighteen shillings in the pound, even if distributed in the most judicious manner, would have a little the same effect as that resulting from the supposition I have just made, and no possible contributions of sacrifices of the rich, particularly in money, could for any time prevent the recurrence of distress among the lower members of society whoever they were. Great changes might, indeed, be made. The rich might become poor, and some of the poor rich, but a part of the society must necessarily feel a difficulty of living, and this difficulty will naturally fall on the least fortunate members.

It may at first appear strange, but I believe it is true, that I cannot by means of money raise a poor man and enable him to live much better than he did before, without proportionably depressing others in the same class. If I retrench the quantity of food consumed in my house, and give him what I have cut off,

I then benefit him, without depressing any but myself and family, who, perhaps, may be well able to bear it. If I turn up a piece of uncultivated land, and give him the produce, I then benefit both him and all the members of the society, because what he before consumed is thrown into the common stock, and probably some of the new produce with it. But if I only give him money, supposing the produce of the country to remain the same, I give him a title to a larger share of that produce than formerly, which share he cannot receive without diminishing the shares of others. It is evident that this effect, in individual instances, must be so small as to be totally imperceptible; but still it must exist, as many other effects do, which like some of the insects that people the air, elude our grosser perceptions.

Supposing the quantity of food in any country to remain the same for many years together, it is evident that this food must be divided according to the value of each man's patent,* or the sum of money that he can afford to spend in this commodity so universally in request. It is a demonstrative truth, therefore, that the patents of one set of men could not be increased in value without diminishing the value of the patents of some other set of men. If the rich were to subscribe and give five shillings a day to five hundred thousand men without retrenching their own tables, no doubt can exist, that as these men would naturally live more at their ease and consume a greater quantity of provisions, there would be less food remaining to divide among the rest, and consequently each man's patent would be diminished in value or the same number of pieces of silver would purchase a smaller quantity of subsistence.

An increase of population without a proportional increase of food will evidently have the same effect in lowering the value of each man's patent. The food must necessarily be distributed in smaller quantities, and consequently a day's labour will purchase a smaller quantity of provisions. An increase in the price of provisions would arise either from an increase of population faster

* Mr. Godwin calls the wealth that a man receives from his ancestors a mouldy patent. It may, I think, very properly be termed a patent, but I hardly see the propriety of calling it a mouldy one, as it is an article in such constant use.

than the means of subsistence, or from a different distribution of
the money of the society. The food of a country that has been long
occupied, if it be increasing, increases slowly and regularly and,
cannot be made to answer any sudden demands, but variations in
the distribution of the money of a society are not unfrequently
occurring, and are undoubtedly among the causes that occasion
the continual variations which we observe in the price of provisions.

The poor-laws of England tend to depress the general condition
of the poor in these two ways. Their first obvious tendency is to
increase population without increasing the food for its support.
A poor man may marry with little or no prospect of being able to
support a family in independence. They may be said therefore in
some measure to create the poor which they maintain, and as the
provisions of the country must, in consequence of the increased
population, be distributed to every man in smaller proportions,
it is evident that the labour of those who are not supported by
parish assistance will purchase a smaller quantity of provisions
than before and consequently more of them must be driven to
ask for support.

Secondly, the quantity of provisions consumed in workhouses
upon a part of the society that cannot in general be considered as
the most valuable part diminishes the shares that would otherwise
belong to more industrious and more worthy members, and thus
in the same manner forces more to become dependent. If the poor
in the workhouses were to live better than they now do, this new
distribution of the money of the society would tend more con-
spicuously to depress the condition of those out of the workhouses
by occasioning a rise in the price of provisions.

Fortunately for England, a spirit of independence still remains
among the peasantry. The poor-laws are strongly calculated to
eradicate this spirit. They have succeeded in part, but had they
succeeded as completely as might have been expected their per-
nicious tendency would not have been so long concealed.

Hard as it may appear in individual instances, dependent
poverty ought to be held disgraceful. Such a stimulus seems to be
absolutely necessary to promote the happiness of the great mass
of mankind, and every general attempt to weaken this stimulus,

however benevolent its apparent intention, will always defeat its own purpose. If men are induced to marry from a prospect of parish provision, with little or no chance of maintaining their families in independence, they are not only unjustly tempted to bring unhappiness and dependence upon themselves and children, but they are tempted, without knowing it, to injure all in the same class with themselves. A labourer who marries without being able to support a family may in some respects be considered as an enemy to all his fellow-labourers.

I feel no doubt whatever that the parish laws of England have contributed to raise the price of provisions and to lower the real price of labour. They have therefore contributed to impoverish that class of people whose only possession is their labour. It is also difficult to suppose that they have not powerfully contributed to generate that carelessness and want of frugality observable among the poor, so contrary to the disposition frequently to be remarked among petty tradesmen and small farmers. The labouring poor, to use a vulgar expression, seem always to live from hand to mouth. Their present wants employ their whole attention, and they seldom think of the future. Even when they have an opportunity of saving they seldom exercise it, but all that is beyond their present necessities goes, generally speaking, to the ale-house. The poor-laws of England may therefore be said to diminish both the power and the will to save among the common people, and thus to weaken one of the strongest incentives to sobriety and industry, and consequently to happiness.

It is a general complaint among master manufacturers that high wages ruin all their workmen, but it is difficult to conceive that these men would not save a part of their high wages for the future support of their families, instead of spending it in drunkenness and dissipation, if they did not rely on parish assistance for support in case of accidents. And that the poor employed in manufactures consider this assistance as a reason why they may spend all the wages they earn and enjoy themselves while they can appears to be evident from the number of families that, upon the failure of any great manufactory, immediately fall upon the parish, when perhaps the wages earned in this manufactory while it flourished were sufficiently above the price of common country labour to have allowed them to save enough for their support till they could find some other channel for their industry.

A man who might not be deterred from going to the ale-house from the consideration that on his death, or sickness, he should leave his wife and family upon the parish might yet hesitate in thus dissipating his earnings if he were assured that, in either of these cases, his family must starve or be left to the support of casual bounty. In China, where the real as well as nominal price of labour is very low, sons are yet obliged by law to support their aged and helpless parents. Whether such a law would be adviseable in this country I will not pretend to determine. But it seems at any rate highly improper, by positive institutions, which render dependent poverty so general, to weaken that disgrace, which for the best and most humane reasons ought to attach to it.

The mass of happiness among the common people cannot but be diminished, when one of the strongest checks to idleness and dissipation is thus removed, and when men are thus allured to marry with little or no prospect of being able to maintain a family in independence. Every obstacle in the way of marriage must undoubtedly be considered as a species of unhappiness. But as from the laws of our nature some check to population must exist, it is better that it should be checked from a foresight of the difficulties attending a family and the fear of dependent poverty than that it should be encouraged, only to be repressed afterwards by want and sickness.

It should be remembered always that there is an essential difference between food and those wrought commodities, the raw materials of which are in great plenty. A demand for these last will not fail to create them in as great a quantity as they are wanted. The demand for food has by no means the same creative power. In a country where all the fertile spots have been seized, high offers are necessary to encourage the farmer to lay his dressing on land from which he cannot expect a profitable return for some years. And before the prospect of advantage is sufficiently great to encourage this sort of agricultural enterprize, and while the new produce is rising, great distresses may be suffered from the want of it. The demand for an increased quantity of subsistence is, with few exceptions, constant every where, yet we see how slowly it is answered in all those countries that have been long occupied.

The poor-laws of England were undoubtedly instituted for the most benevolent purpose, but there is great reason to think that they have not succeeded in their intention. They certainly mitigate some cases of very severe distress which might otherwise occur, yet the state of the poor who are supported by parishes, considered in all its circumstances, is very far from being free from misery. But one of the principal objections to them is that for this assistance which some of the poor receive, in itself almost a doubtful blessing, the whole class of the common people of England is subjected to a set of grating, inconvenient, and tyrannical laws, totally inconsistent with the genuine spirit of the constitution. The whole business of settlements, even in its present amended state, is utterly contradictory to all ideas of freedom. The parish persecution of men whose families are likely to become chargeable, and of poor women who are near lying-in, is a most disgraceful and disgusting tyranny. And the obstructions continually occasioned in the market of labour by these laws, have a constant tendency to add to the difficulties of those who are struggling to support themselves without assistance.

These evils attendant on the poor-laws are in some degree irremediable. If assistance be to be distributed to a certain class of people, a power must be given somewhere of discriminating the proper objects and of managing the concerns of the institutions that are necessary, but any great interference with the affairs of other people, is a species of tyranny, and in the common course of things the exercise of this power may be expected to become grating to those who are driven to ask for support. The tyranny of Justices, Churchwardens, and Overseers, is a common complaint among the poor, but the fault does not lie so much in these persons, who probably before they were in power, were not worse than other people, but in the nature of all such institutions.

The evil is perhaps gone too far to be remedied, but I feel little doubt in my own mind that if the poor-laws had never existed, though there might have been a few more instances of very severe distress, yet that the aggregate mass of happiness among the common people would have been much greater than it is at present.

Mr. Pitt's Poor-bill has the appearance of being framed with benevolent intentions, and the clamour raised against it was in many respects ill directed, and unreasonable. But it must be confessed that it possesses in a high degree the great and radical defect of all systems of the kind, that of tending to increase population without increasing the means for its support, and thus to depress the condition of those that are not supported by parishes, and, consequently, to create more poor.

To remove the wants of the lower classes of society is indeed an arduous task. The truth is that the pressure of distress on this part of a community is an evil so deeply seated that no human ingenuity can reach it. Were I to propose a palliative, and palliatives are all that the nature of the case will admit, it should be, in the first place, the total abolition of all the present parish-laws. This would at any rate give liberty and freedom of action to the peasantry of England, which they can hardly be said to possess at present. They would then be able to settle without interruption, wherever there was a prospect of a greater plenty of work and a higher price for labour. The market of labour would then be free, and those obstacles removed, which as things are now, often for a considerable time prevent the price from rising according to the demand.

Secondly, Premiums might be given for turning up fresh land, and all possible encouragements held out to agriculture above manufactures, and to tillage above grazing. Every endeavour should be used to weaken and destroy all those institutions relating to corporations, apprenticeships, &c, which cause the labours of agriculture to be worse paid than the labours of trade and manufactures. For a country can never produce its proper quantity of food while these distinctions remain in favour of artizans. Such encouragements to agriculture would tend to furnish the market with an increasing quantity of healthy work, and at the same time, by augmenting the produce of the country, would raise the comparative price of labour and ameliorate the condition of the labourer. Being now in better circumstances, and seeing no prospect of parish assistance, he would be more able, as well as more inclined, to enter into associations for providing against the sickness of himself or family.

Lastly, for cases of extreme distress, county workhouses might be established, supported by rates upon the whole kingdom, and free for persons of all counties, and indeed of all nations. The fare should be hard, and those that were able obliged to work. It would be desireable that they should not be considered as comfortable asylums in all difficulties, but merely as places where severe distress might find some alleviation. A part of these houses might be separated, or others built for a most beneficial purpose, which has not been unfrequently taken notice of, that of providing a place where any person, whether native or foreigner, might do a day's work at all times and receive the market price for it. Many cases would undoubtedly be left for the exertion of individual benevolence.

A plan of this kind, the preliminary of which should be an abolition of all the present parish laws, seems to be the best calculated to increase the mass of happiness among the common people of England. To prevent the recurrence of misery, is, alas! beyond the power of man. In the vain endeavour to attain what in the nature of things is impossible, we now sacrifice not only possible but certain benefits. We tell the common people that if they will submit to a code of tyrannical regulations, they shall never be in want. They do submit to these regulations. They perform their part of the contract, but we do not, nay cannot, perform ours, and thus the poor sacrifice the valuable blessing of liberty and receive nothing that can be called an equivalent in return.

Notwithstanding then, the institution of the poor-laws in England, I think it will be allowed that considering the state of the lower classes altogether, both in the towns and in the country, the distresses which they suffer from the want of proper and sufficient food, from hard labour and unwholesome habitations, must operate as a constant check to incipient population.

To these two great checks to population, in all long occupied countries, which I have called the preventive and the positive checks, may be added, vicious customs with respect to women, great cities, unwholesome manufactures, luxury, pestilence, and war.

All these checks may be fairly resolved into misery and vice.

And that these are the true causes of the slow increase of population in all the states of modern Europe, will appear sufficiently evident from the comparatively rapid increase that has invariably taken place whenever these causes have been in any considerable degree removed.

CHAPTER VI

It has been universally remarked that all new colonies settled in healthy countries, where there was plenty of room and food, have constantly increased with astonishing rapidity in their population. Some of the colonies from ancient Greece, in no very long period, more than equalled their parent states in numbers and strength. And not to dwell on remote instances, the European settlements in the new world bear ample testimony to the truth of a remark, which, indeed, has never, that I know of, been doubted. A plenty of rich land, to be had for little or nothing, is so powerful a cause of population as to overcome all other obstacles. No settlements could well have been worse managed than those of Spain in Mexico, Peru, and Quito. The tyranny, superstition, and vices, of the mother-country, were introduced in ample quantities among her children. Exorbitant taxes were exacted by the Crown. The most arbitrary restrictions were imposed on their trade. And the governors were not behind hand in rapacity and extortion for themselves as well as their master. Yet, under all these difficulties, the colonies made a quick progress in population. The city of Lima, founded since the conquest, is represented by Ulloa as containing fifty thousand inhabitants near fifty years ago. Quito, which had been but a hamlet of Indians, is represented by the same author as in his time equally populous. Mexico is said to contain a hundred thousand inhabitants, which, notwithstanding the exaggerations of the Spanish writers, is supposed to be five times greater than what it contained in the time of Montezuma.

In the Portuguese colony of Brazil, governed with almost equal tyranny, there were supposed to be, thirty years since, six hundred thousand inhabitants of European extraction.

The Dutch and French colonies, though under the government of exclusive companies of merchants, which, as Dr. Adam Smith says very justly, is the worst of all possible governments, still persisted in thriving under every disadvantage.

But the English North American colonies, now the powerful People of the United States of America, made by far the most rapid progress. To the plenty of good land which they possessed in common with the Spanish and Portuguese settlements, they added a greater degree of liberty and equality. Though not without some restrictions on their foreign commerce, they were allowed a perfect liberty of managing their own internal affairs. The political institutions that prevailed were favourable to the alienation and division of property. Lands that were not cultivated by the proprietor within a limited time were declared grantable to any other person. In Pennsylvania there was no right of primogeniture, and in the provinces of New England the eldest had only a double share. There were no tythes in any of the States, and scarcely any taxes. And on account of the extreme cheapness of good land a capital could not be more advantageously employed than in agriculture which at the same time that it supplies the greatest quantity of healthy work affords much the most valuable produce to the society.

The consequence of these favourable circumstances united was a rapidity of increase, probably without parallel in history. Throughout all the northern colonies, the population was found to double itself in 25 years. The original number of persons who had settled in the four provinces of new England in 1643, was 21,200.* Afterwards, it is supposed that more left them than went to them. In the year 1760, they were increased to half a million. They had therefore all along doubled their own number in 25 years. In New Jersey the period of doubling appeared to be 22 years; and in Rhode Island still less. In the back settlements, where the inhabitants applied themselves solely to agriculture, and luxury was not known, they were found to double their own

---

* I take these facts from Dr. Price's two volumes of Observations, not having Dr. Styles's pamphlet, from which he quotes, by me.

number in 15 years, a most extraordinary instance of increase.*
Along the sea coast, which would naturally be first inhabited, the
period of doubling was about 35 years; and in some of the mari-
time towns, the population was absolutely at a stand.

These facts seem to shew that population increases exactly
in the proportion, that the two great checks to it, misery and vice,
are removed and that there is not a truer criterion of the happiness
and innocence of a people than the rapidity of their increase. The
unwholesomeness of towns, to which some persons are necessarily
driven from the nature of their trades, must be considered as a
species of misery, and every the slightest check to marriage, from a
prospect of the difficulty of maintaining a family, may be fairly
classed under the same head. I nshort it is difficult to conceive any
check to population which does not come under the description of
some species of misery or vice.

The population of the thirteen American States before the war,
was reckoned at about three millions. Nobody imagines that Great
Britain is less populous at present for the emigration of the small
parent stock that produced these numbers. On the contrary, a
certain degree of emigration is known to be favourable to the
population of the mother country. It has been particularly remarked that the two Spanish provinces from which the greatest
number of people emigrated to America, became in consequence
more populous. Whatever was the original number of British

---

* In instances of this kind the powers of the earth appear to be fully equal
to answer all the demands for food that can be made upon it by man. But we
should be led into an error if we were thence to suppose that population and
food ever really increase in the same ratio. The one is still a geometrical and
the other an arithmetical ratio, that is, one increases by multiplication, and the
other by addition. Where there are few people, and a great quantity of fertile
land, the power of the earth to afford a yearly increase of food may be compared
to a great reservoir of water, supplied by a moderate stream. The faster population increases, the more help will be got to draw off the water, and consequently
an increasing quantity will be taken every year. But the sooner, undoubtedly,
will the reservoir be exhausted, and the streams only remain. When acre has
been added to acre, till all the fertile land is occupied, the yearly increase of
food will depend upon the amelioration of the land already in possession; and
even this moderate stream will be gradually diminishing. But population, could
it be supplied with food, would go on with unexhausted vigour, and the increase
of one period would furnish the power of a greater increase the next, and this
without any limit.

Emigrants that increased so fast in the North American Colonies, let us ask, why does not an equal number produce an equal increase in the same time in Great Britain? The great and obvious cause to be assigned is the want of room and food, or, in other words, misery, and that this is a much more powerful cause even than vice appears sufficiently evident from the rapidity with which even old States recover the desolations of war, pestilence, or the accidents of nature. They are then for a short time placed a little in the situation of new states, and the effect is always answerable to what might be expected. If the industry of the inhabitants be not destroyed by fear or tyranny, subsistence will soon increase beyond the wants of the reduced numbers, and the invariable consequence will be, that population which before, perhaps, was nearly stationary, will begin immediately to increaese.

The fertile province of Flanders, which has been so often the seat of the most destructive wars, after a respite of a few years, has appeared always as fruitful and as populous as ever. Even the Palatinate lifted up its head again after the execrable ravages of Louis the Fourteenth. The effects of the dreadful plague in London in 1666 were not perceptible 15 or 20 years afterwards. The traces of the most destructive famines in China and Indostan are by all accounts very soon obliterated. It may even be doubted whether Turkey and Egypt are upon an average much less populous, for the plagues that periodically lay them waste. If the number of people which they contain be less now than formerly, it is, probably, rather to be attributed to the tyranny and oppression of the government under which they groan, and the consequent discouragements to agriculture, than to the loss which they sustain by the plague. The most tremendous convulsions of nature, such as volcanic eruptions and earthquakes, if they do not happen so frequently as to drive away the inhabitants, or to destroy their spirit of industry, have but a trifling effect on the average population of any state. Naples, and the country under Vesuvius, are still very populous, notwithstanding the repeated eruptions of that mountain. And Lisbon and Lima are now, probably, nearly in the same state with regard to population, as they were before the last earthquakes.

CHAPTER VII

By great attention to cleanliness, the plague seems at length to be completely expelled from London. But it is not improbable that among the secondary causes that produce even sickly seasons and epidemics ought to be ranked a crowded population and unwholesome and insufficient food. I have been led to this remark, by looking over some of the tables of Mr. Susmilch, which Dr. Price has extracted in one of his notes to the postscript on the controversy respecting the population of England and Wales. They are considered as very correct, and if such tables were general, they would throw great light on the different ways by which population is repressed and prevented from increasing beyond the means of subsistence in any country. I will extract a part of the tables, with Dr. Price's remarks.

IN THE KINGDOM OF PRUSSIA, AND DUKEDOM OF LITHUANIA

Annual Average	Births	Burials	Marriages	Proportion of Births to Marriages	Proportion of Births to Burials
10 Yrs. to 1702	21963	14718	5928	37 to 10	150 to 100
5 Yrs. to 1716	21602	11984	4968	37 to 10	180 to 100
5 Yrs. to 1756	28392	19154	5599	50 to 10	148 to 100

"N. B. In 1709 and 1710, a pestilence carried off 247,733 of the inhabitants of this country, and in 1736 and 1737, epidemics prevailed, which again checked its increase."

It may be remarked, that the greatest proportion of births to burials, was in the five years after the great pestilence.

DUTCHY OF POMERANIA

Annual Average	Births	Burials	Marriages	Proportion of Births to Marriages	Proportion of Births to Burials
6 Yrs. to 1702	6540	4647	1810	36 to 10	140 to 100
6 Yrs. to 1708	7455	4208	1875	39 to 10	177 to 100
6 Yrs. to 1726	8432	5627	2131	39 to 10	150 to 100
4 Yrs. to 1756	12767	9281	2957	43 to 10	137 to 100

"In this instance the inhabitants appear to have been almost doubled in 56 years, no very bad epidemics having once interrupted the increase, but the three years immediately following the last period (to 1759) were years so sickly that the births were sunk to 10,229, and the burials raised to 15,068."

Is it not probable that in this case the number of inhabitants had increased faster than the food and the accommodations necessary to preserve them in health? The mass of the people would, upon this supposition, be obliged to live harder, and a greater number would be crowded together in one house, and it is not surely improbable that these were among the natural causes that produced the three sickly years. These causes may produce such an effect, though the country, absolutely considered, may not be extremely crowded and populous. In a country even thinly inhabited, if an increase of population take place, before more food is raised, and more houses are built, the inhabitants must be distressed in some degree for room and subsistence. Were the marriages in England, for the next eight or ten years, to be more prolifick than usual, or even were a greater number of marriages than usual to take place, supposing the number of houses to remain the same, instead of five or six to a cottage, there must be seven or eight, and this, added to the necessity of harder living, would probably have a very unfavourable effect on the health of the common people.

NEUMARK OF BRANDENBURGH

Annual Average	Births	Burials	Marriages	Proportion of Births to Marriages	Proportion of Births to Burials
5 Yrs. to 1701	5433	3483	1436	37 to 10	155 to 100
5 Yrs. to 1726	7012	4254	1713	40 to 10	164 to 100
5 Yrs. to 1756	7978	5567	1891	42 to 10	143 to 100

"Epidemics prevailed for six years, from 1736, to 1741, which checked the increase."

DUKEDOM OF MAGDEBURGH

Annual Average	Births	Burials	Marriages	Proportion of Births to Marriages	Proportion of Births to Burials
5 Yrs. to 1702	6431	4103	1681	38 to 10	156 to 100
5 Yrs. to 1717	7590	5335	2076	36 to 10	142 to 100
5 Yrs. to 1756	8850	8069	2193	40 to 10	109 to 100

"The years 1738, 1740, 1750, and 1751, were particularly sickly."

For further information on this subject, I refer the reader to Mr. Susmilch's tables. The extracts that I have made are sufficient to shew the periodical, though irregular returns of sickly seasons, and it seems highly probable, that a scantiness of room and food was one of the principal causes that occasioned them.

It appears from the tables that these countries were increasing rather fast for old states, notwithstanding the occasional sickly seasons that prevailed. Cultivation must have been improving, and marriages, consequently, encouraged. For the checks to population appear to have been rather of the positive, than of the preventive kind. When from a prospect of increasing plenty in any country, the weight that represses population is in some degree removed, it is highly probable that the motion will be continued beyond the operation of the cause that first impelled it. Or, to be more particular, when the increasing produce of a country, and the increasing demand for labour, so far ameliorate the condition of the labourer, as greatly to encourage marriage, it is probable that the custom of early marriages will continue till the population of the country has gone beyond the increased produce, and sickly seasons appear to be the natural and necessary consequence. I should expect, therefore, that those countries where subsistence was increasing sufficiently at times to encourage population but not to answer all its demands, would be more subject to periodical epidemics than those where the population could more completely accommodate itself to the average produce.

An observation the converse of this will probably also be found true. In those countries that are subject to periodical sicknesses, the increase of population, or the excess of births above the burials, will be greater in the intervals of these periods, than is usual, caeteris paribus, in the countries not so much subject to such disorders. If Turkey and Egypt have been nearly stationary in their average population for the last century, in the intervals of their periodical plagues, the births must have exceeded the burials in a greater proportion than in such countries as France and England.

The average proportion of births to burials in any country for a period of five or ten years, will hence appear to be a very inadequate criterion by which to judge of its real progress in population. This proportion certainly shews the rate of increase during those five or ten years; but we can by no means thence infer, what had been the increase for the twenty years before, or what would be the increase for the twenty years after. Dr. Price observes, that Sweden, Norway, Russia, and the kingdom of Naples, are increasing fast; but the extracts from registers that he has given, are not for periods of sufficient extent to establish the fact. It is highly probable, however, that Sweden, Norway, and Russia, are really increasing in their population, though not at the rate that the proportion of births to burials for the short periods that Dr. Price takes would seem to shew.* For five years, ending in 1777, the proportion of births to burials in the kingdom of Naples was 144 to 100, but there is reason to suppose that this proportion would indicate an increase much greater than would be really found to have taken place in that kingdom during a period of a hundred years.

Dr. Short compared the registers of many villages and market towns in England for two periods; the first, from Queen Elizabeth to the middle of the last century, and the second, from different years at the end of the last century, to the middle of the present. And from a comparison of these extracts, it appears that in the former period the births exceeded the burials in the proportion of 124 to 100, but in the latter, only in the proportion of 111 to 100. Dr. Price thinks that the registers in the former period are not to be depended upon, but, probably, in this instance they do not give incorrect proportions. At least there are many reasons for expecting to find a greater excess of births above the burials in the former period than in the latter. In the natural progress of the population of any country, more good land will, caeteris paribus,† be taken into cultivation in the earlier stages of it than in the

---

* See Dr. Price's Observations, 2 Vol. Postscript to the controversy on the population of England and Wales.

† I say caeteris paribus, because the increase of the produce of any country will always very greatly depend on the spirit of industry that prevails, and the way in which it is directed. The knowledge and habits of the people, and other temporary causes, particularly the degree of civil liberty and equality existing at the time, must always have great influence in exciting and directing this spirit.

later. And a greater proportional yearly increase of produce, will almost invariably be followed by a greater proportional increase of population. But, besides this great cause, which would naturally give the excess of births above the burials greater at the end of Queen Elizabeth's reign, than in the middle of the present century, I cannot help thinking that the occasional ravages of the plague in the former period, must have had some tendency to increase this proportion. If an average of ten years had been taken in the intervals of the returns of this dreadful disorder; or if the years of plague had been rejected as accidental, the registers would certainly give the proportion of births to burials too high for the real average increase of the population. For some few years after the great plague in 1666, it is probable that there was a more than usual excess of births above burials, particularly if Dr. Price's opinion be founded, that England was more populous at the revolution (which happened only 22 years afterwards) than it is at present.

Mr. King, in 1693, stated the proportion of the births to the burials throughout the Kingdom, exclusive of London, as 115 to 100. Dr. Short makes it, in the middle of the present century, 111 to 100, including London. The proportion in France for five years, ending in 1774, was 117 to 100. If these statements are near the truth; and if there are no very great variations at particular periods in the proportions, it would appear, that the population of France and England has accommodated itself very nearly to the average produce of each country. The discouragements to marriage, the consequent vicious habits, war, luxury, the silent though certain depopulation of large towns, and the close habitations, and insufficient food of many of the poor, prevent population from increasing beyond the means of subsistence; and, if I may use an expression which certainly at first appears strange, supercede the necessity of great and ravaging epidemics to repress what is redundant. Were a wasting plague to sweep off two millions in England, and six millions in France, there can be no doubt whatever, that after the inhabitants had recovered from the dreadful shock, the proportion of births to burials would be much above what it is in either country at present.

In New Jersey, the proportion of births to deaths on an average of seven years, ending in 1743, was as 300 to 100. In France and England, taking the highest proportion, it is as 117 to 100. Great and astonishing as this difference is, we ought not to be so wonder-struck at it, as to attribute it to the miraculous interposition of heaven. The causes of it are not remote, latent and mysterious; but near us, round about us, and open to the investigation of every inquiring mind. It accords with the most liberal spirit of philos-ophy, to suppose that not a stone can fall, or a plant rise, without the immediate agency of divine power. But we know from experi-ence, that these operations of what we call nature have been con-ducted almost invariably according to fixed laws. And since the world began, the causes of population and depopulation have probably been as constant as any of the laws of nature with which we are acquainted.

The passion between the sexes has appeared in every age to be so nearly the same that it may always be considered, in algebraic language, as a given quantity. The great law of necessity which prevents population from increasing in any country beyond the food which it can either produce or acquire, is a law, so open to our view, so obvious and evident to our understandings, and so completely confirmed by the experience of every age, that we can-not for a moment doubt it. The different modes which nature takes to prevent or repress a redundant population, do not appear, indeed, to us so certain and regular, but though we cannot always predict the mode we may with certainty predict the fact. If the proportion of births to deaths for a few years, indicate an increase of numbers much beyond the proportional increased or acquired produce of the country, we may be perfectly certain that unless an emigration takes place, the deaths will shortly exceed the births; and that the increase that had taken place for a few years cannot be the real average increase of the population of the country. Were there no other depopulating causes, every country would, without doubt, be subject to periodical pestilences or famines.

The only true criterion of a real and permanent increase in the population of any country is the increase of the means of sub-sistence. But even this criterion is subject to some slight variations which are, however, completely open to our view and observations. In some countries population appears to have been forced, that is, the people have been habituated by degrees to live almost upon the smallest possible quantity of food. There must have been periods in such countries when population increased permanently, without an increase in the means of subsistence. China seems to answer to this description. If the accounts we have of it are to be trusted, the lower classes of people are in the habit of living almost upon the smallest possible quantity of food and are glad to get any putrid offals that European labourers would rather starve than eat. The law in China which permits parents to expose their children has tended principally thus to force the population. A nation in this state must necessarily be subject to famines. Where a country is so populous in proportion to the means of subsistence that the average produce of it is but barely sufficient to support the lives of the inhabitants, any deficiency from the badness of seasons must be fatal. It is probable that the very frugal manner in which the Gentoos are in the habit of living contributes in some degree to the famines of Indostan.

In America, where the reward of labour is at present so liberal, the lower classes might retrench very considerably in a year of scarcity without materially distressing themselves. A famine therefore seems to be almost impossible. It may be expected that in the progress of the population of America, the labourers will in time be much less liberally rewarded. The numbers will in this case permanently increase without a proportional increase in the means of subsistence.

In the different States of Europe there must be some variations in the proportion between the number of inhabitants and the quantity of food consumed, arising from the different habits of living that prevail in each State. The labourers of the South of England are so accustomed to eat fine wheaten bread that they will suffer themselves to be half starved before they will submit to live like the Scotch peasants. They might perhaps in time, by the constant operation of the hard law of necessity, be reduced to live even like the lower Chinese, and the country would then, with the same quantity of food, support a greater population. But to effect this must always be a most difficult, and every friend to humanity will hope, an abortive attempt. Nothing is so common as to hear of encouragements that ought to be given to population. If the tendency of mankind to increase be so great as I have represented it to be, it may appear strange that this increase does not come when it is thus repeatedly called for. The true reason is that the demand for a greater population is made without preparing the funds necessary to support it. Increase the demand for agricultural labour by promoting cultivation, and with it consequently increase the produce of the country, and ameliorate the condition of the labourer, and no apprehensions whatever need be entertained of the proportional increase of population. An attempt to effect this purpose in any other way is vicious, cruel, and tyrannical, and in any state of tolerable freedom cannot therefore succeed. It may appear to be the interest of the rulers, and the rich of a State, to force population, and thereby lower the price of labour, and consequently the expense of fleets and armies, and the cost of manufactures for foreign sale, but every attempt of the kind should be carefully watched and strenuously resisted by the friends of the poor, particularly when it comes under the deceitful garb of benevolence, and is likely, on that account, to be cheerfully, and cordially received by the common people.

I entirely acquit Mr. Pitt of any sinister intention in that clause of his poor bill which allows a shilling a week to every labourer for each child he has above three. I confess, that before the bill was brought into Parliament, and for some time after, I thought that such a regulation would be highly beneficial, but further reflection on the subject has convinced me that if its object be to better the condition of the poor, it is calculated to defeat the very purpose which it has in view. It has no tendency that I can discover to increase the produce of the country, and if it tend to increase the population, without increasing the produce, the necessary and inevitable consequence appears to be that the same produce must be divided among a greater number, and consequently that a day's labour will purchase a smaller quantity of provisions, and the poor therefore in general must be more distressed.

I have mentioned some cases, where population may permanently increase, without a proportional increase in the means of subsistence. But it is evident that the variation in different States, between the food and the numbers supported by it, is restricted to a limit beyond which it cannot pass. In every country, the population of which is not absolutely decreasing, the food must be necessarily sufficient to support, and to continue, the race of labourers.

Other circumstances being the same, it may be affirmed that countries are populous according to the quantity of human food which they produce, and happy according to the liberality with which that food is divided, or the quantity which a day's labour will purchase. Corn countries are more populous than pasture countries, and rice countries more populous than corn countries. The lands in England are not suited to rice, but they would all bear potatoes; and Dr. Adam Smith observes that if potatoes were to become the favourite vegetable food of the common people, and if the same quantity of land was employed in their culture as is now employed in the culture of corn, the country would be able to support a much greater population, and would consequently in a very short time have it.

The happiness of a country does not depend, absolutely, upon its poverty or its riches, upon its youth or its age, upon its being thinly or fully inhabited, but upon the rapidity with which it is increasing, upon the degree in which the yearly increase of food approaches to the yearly increase of an unrestricted population. This approximation is always the nearest in new colonies, where the knowledge and industry of an old State, operate on the fertile unappropriated land of a new one. In other cases, the youth or the age of a State is not in this respect of very great importance. It is probable, that the food of Great Britain is divided in as great plenty to the inhabitants, at the present period, as it was two thousand, three thousand, or four thousand years ago. And there is reason to believe that the poor and thinly inhabited tracts of the Scotch Highlands, are as much distressed by an overcharged population, as the rich and populous province of Flanders.

Were a country never to be over-run by a people more advanced in arts, but left to its own natural progress in civilization; from the time that its produce might be considered as an unit, to the time that it might be considered as a million, during the lapse of many hundred years, there would not be a single period, when the mass of the people could be said to be free from distress, either directly or indirectly, for want of food. In every State in Europe, since we have first had accounts of it, millions and millions of human existences have been repressed from this simple cause; though perhaps in some of these States, an absolute famine has never been known.

Famine seems to be the last, the most dreadful resource of nature. The power of population is so superior to the power in the earth to produce subsistence for man, that premature death must in some shape or other visit the human race. The vices of mankind are active and able ministers of depopulation. They are the precursors in the great army of destruction; and often finish the dreadful work themselves. But should they fail in this war of extermination, sickly seasons, epidemics, pestilence, and plague, advance in terrific array, and sweep off their thousands and ten thousands. Should success be still incomplete, gigantic inevitable famine stalks in the rear, and with one mighty blow, levels the population with the food of the world.

Must it not then be acknowledged by an attentive examiner of the histories of mankind, that in every age and in every State in which man has existed, or does now exist,

That the increase of population is necessarily limited by the means of subsistence.

That population does invariably increase when the means of subsistence increase. And, that the superior power of population is repressed, and the actual population kept equal to the means of subsistence by misery and vice.

CHAPTER VIII

To a person who draws the preceding obvious inferences, from a view of the past and present state of mankind, it cannot but be a matter of astonishment that all the writers on the perfectibility of man and of society who have noticed the argument of an overcharged population, treat it always very slightly and invariably represent the difficulties arising from it as at a great and almost immeasurable distance. Even Mr. Wallace, who thought the argument itself of so much weight as to destroy his whole system of equality, did not seem to be aware that any difficulty would occur from this cause till the whole earth had been cultivated like a garden and was incapable of any further increase of produce. Were this really the case, and were a beautiful system of equality in other respects practicable, I cannot think that our ardour in the pursuit of such a scheme ought to be damped by the contemplation of so remote a difficulty. An event at such a distance might fairly be left to providence, but the truth is that if the view of the argument given in this essay be just the difficulty, so far from being remote, would be imminent and immediate. At every period during the progress of cultivation, from the present moment to the time when the whole earth was become like a garden, the distress for want of food would be constantly pressing on all mankind, if they were equal. Though the produce of the earth might be increasing every year, population would be increasing much faster, and the redundancy must necessarily be repressed by the periodical or constant action of misery or vice.

Mr. Condorcet's Esquisse d'un tableau historique des progrès de l'esprit humain, was written, it is said, under the pressure of that cruel proscription which terminated in his death. If he had no hopes of its being seen during his life and of its interesting France in his favour, it is a singular instance of the attachment of a man to principles, which every day's experience was so fatally for himself contradicting. To see the human mind in one of the most enlightened nations of the world, and after a lapse of some thousand years, debased by such a fermentation of disgusting passions, of fear, cruelty, malice, revenge, ambition, madness, and folly as would have disgraced the most savage nation in the most barbarous age must have been such a tremendous shock to his ideas of the necessary and inevitable progress of the human mind that nothing but the firmest conviction of the truth of his principles, in spite of all appearances, could have withstood.

This posthumous publication is only a sketch of a much larger work, which he proposed should be executed. It necessarily, therefore, wants that detail and application which can alone prove the truth of any theory. A few observations will be sufficient to shew how completely the theory is contradicted when it is applied to the real, and not to an imaginary, state of things.

In the last division of the work, which treats of the future progress of man towards perfection, he says, that comparing, in the different civilized nations of Europe, the actual population with the extent of territory, and observing their cultivation, their industry, their divisions of labour, and their means of subsistence, we shall see that it would be impossible to preserve the same means of subsistence, and, consequently, the same population, without a number of individuals who have no other means of supplying their wants than their industry. Having allowed the necessity of such a class of men, and adverting afterwards to the precarious revenue of those families that would depend so entirely on the life and health of their chief,* he says, very justly, "There exists then, a necessary cause of inequality, of dependence, and even of misery, which menaces, without ceasing, the most numerous and active class of our societies." The difficulty is just and well stated, and I am afraid that the mode by which he proposes it should be removed, will be found inefficacious. By the application of calcula-

---

* To save time and long quotations, I shall here give the substance of some of Mr. Condorcet's sentiments, and hope I shall not misrepresent them, but I refer the reader to the work itself, which will amuse, if it does not convince him.

tions to the probabilities of life and the interest of money, he proposes that a fund should be established which should assure to the old an assistance, produced, in part, by their own former savings, and, in part, by the savings of individuals who in making the same sacrifice die before they reap the benefit of it. The same, or a similar fund, should give assistance to women and children who lose their husbands, or fathers and afford a capital to those who were of an age to found a new family, sufficient for the proper development of their industry. These establishments he observes, might be made in the name and under the protection of the society. Going still further, he says, that by the just application of calculations, means might be found of more completely preserving a state of equality, by preventing credit from being the exclusive privilege of great fortunes, and yet giving it a basis equally solid, and by rendering the progress of industry, and the activity of commerce, less dependent on great capitalists.

Such establishments and calculations may appear very promising upon paper, but when applied to real life they will be found to be absolutely nugatory. Mr. Condorcet allows that a class of people which maintains itself entirely by industry is necessary to every state. Why does he allow this? No other reason can well be assigned than that he conceives that the labour necessary to procure subsistence for an extended population will not be performed without the goad of necessity. If by establishments of this kind this spur to industry be removed, if the idle and the negligent are placed upon the same footing with regard to their credit, and the future support of their wives and families, as the active and industrious, can we expect to see men exert that animated activity in bettering their condition which now forms the master spring of public prosperity? If an inquisition were to be established to examine the claims of each individual and to determine whether he had or had not exerted himself to the utmost, and to grant or refuse assistance accordingly, this would be little else than a repetition upon a larger scale of the English poor laws and would be completely destructive of the true principles of liberty and equality.

But independent of this great objection to these establishments, and supposing for a moment, that they would give no check to productive industry, by far the greatest difficulty remains yet behind.

Were every man sure of a comfortable provision for a family, almost every man would have one, and were the rising generation free from the "killing frost" of misery, population must rapidly increase. Of this Mr. Condorcet seems to be fully aware himself, and after having described further improvements, he says,

"But in this progress of industry and happiness, each generation will be called to more extended enjoyments, and in consequence, by the physical constitution of the human frame, to an increase in the number of individuals. Must not there arrive a period then, when these laws, equally necessary, shall counteract each other? When the increase of the number of men surpassing their means of subsistence, the necessary result must be either a continual diminution of happiness and population, a movement truly retrograde, or at least, a kind of oscillation between good and evil? In societies arrived at this term, will not this oscillation be a constantly subsisting cause of periodical misery? Will it not mark the limit when all further amelioration will become impossible, and point out that term to the perfectibility of the human race which it may reach in the course of ages, but can never pass?"

He then adds,

"There is no person who does not see how very distant such a period is from us, but shall we ever arrive at it? It is equally impossible to pronounce for or against the future realization of an event which cannot take place but at an era when the human race will have attained improvements, of which we can at present scarcely form a conception."

Mr. Condorcet's picture of what may be expected to happen when the number of men shall surpass the means of their subsistence, is justly drawn. The oscillation which he describes, will certainly take place and will without doubt be a constantly subsisting cause of periodical misery. The only point in which I differ from Mr. Condorcet with regard to this picture is the period when it may be applied to the human race. Mr. Condorcet thinks that it cannot possibly be applicable but at an era extremely distant. If the proportion between the natural increase of population and food which I have given be in any degree near the truth, it will appear, on the contrary, that the period when the number of men surpass their means of subsistence has long since arrived, and that this necessary oscillation, this constantly subsisting cause of periodical misery, has existed ever since we have had any histories of mankind, does exist at present, and will for ever continue to exist, unless some decided change take place in the physical constitution of our nature.

Mr. Condorcet, however, goes on to say that should the period which he conceives to be so distant, ever arrive the human race, and the advocates for the perfectibility of man, need not be alarmed at it. He then proceeds to remove the difficulty in a manner which I profess not to understand. Having observed, that the ridiculous prejudices of superstition would by that time have ceased to throw over morals, a corrupt and degrading austerity, he alludes, either to a promiscuous concubinage, which would prevent breeding, or to something else as unnatural. To remove the difficulty in this way will, surely, in the opinion of most men, be to destroy that virtue and purity of manners, which the advocates of equality, and of the perfectibility of man profess to be the end and object of their views.

CHAPTER IX

The last question which Mr. Condorcet proposes for examination is the organic perfectibility of man. He observes that if the proofs which have been already given and which, in their development will receive greater force in the work itself, are sufficient to establish the indefinite perfectibility of man upon the supposition of the same natural faculties and the same organization which he has at present, what will be the certainty, what the extent of our hope, if this organization, these natural faculties themselves, are suscep tible of amelioration?

From the improvement of medicine, from the use of more wholesome food and habitations, from a manner of living which will improve the strength of the body by exercise without impairing it by excess, from the destruction of the two great causes of the degradation of man, misery, and too great riches, from the gradual removal of transmissible and contagious disorders by the improvement of physical knowledge, rendered more efficacious by the progress of reason and of social order, he infers that though man will not absolutely become immortal, yet that the duration between his birth and natural death will increase without ceasing, will have no assignable term, and may properly be expressed by the word indefinite. He then defines this word to mean either a constant approach to an unlimited extent, without ever reaching it, or an increase in the immensity of ages to an extent greater than any assignable quantity.

But surely the application of this term in either of these senses to the duration of human life is in the highest degree unphilosophical and totally unwarranted by any appearances in the laws of nature. Variations from different causes are essentially distinct from a regular and unretrograde increase. The average duration of human life will to a certain degree vary from healthy or unhealthy climates, from wholesome or unwholesome food, from virtuous or vicious manners, and other causes, but it may be fairly doubted, whether there is really the smallest perceptible advance in the natural duration of human life since first we have had any authentic history of man. The prejudices of all ages have indeed been directly contrary to this supposition, and though I would not lay much stress upon these prejudices, they will in some measure tend to prove that there has been no marked advance in an opposite direction.

It may perhaps be said that the world is yet so young, so completely in its infancy, that it ought not to be expected that any difference should appear so soon.

If this be the case, there is at once an end of all human science. The whole train of reasonings from effects to causes will be destroyed. We may shut our eyes to the book of nature, as it will no longer be of any use to read it. The wildest and most improbable conjectures may be advanced with as much certainty as the most just and sublime theories, founded on careful and reiterated experiments. We may return again to the old mode of philosophizing and make facts bend to systems, instead of establishing systems upon facts. The grand and consistent theory of Newton will be placed upon the same footing as the wild and excentric hypotheses of Descartes. In short, if the laws of nature are thus fickle and inconstant, if it can be affirmed and be believed that they will change, when for ages and ages they have appeared immutable, the human mind will no longer have any incitements to inquiry, but must remain fixed in inactive torpor, or amuse itself only in bewildering dreams and extravagant fancies.

The constancy of the laws of nature and of effects and causes is the foundation of all human knowledge, though far be it from me to say that the same power which framed and executes the laws of nature, may not change them all "in a moment, in the twinkling of an eye." Such a change may undoubtedly happen. All that I mean to say is that it is impossible to infer it from reasoning. If without any previous observable symptoms or indications of a change, we can infer that a change will take place, we may as well make any assertion whatever and think it as unreasonable to be contradicted in affirming that the moon will come in contact with the earth to-morrow, as in saying that the sun will rise at its usual time.

With regard to the duration of human life, there does not appear to have existed from the earliest ages of the world to the present moment the smallest permanent symptom or indication of increasing prolongation.* The observable effects of climate, habit, diet, and other causes, on length of life have furnished the pretext for asserting its indefinite extension; and the sandy foundation on which the argument rests, is that because the limit of human life is undefined; because you cannot mark its precise term, and say so far exactly shall it go and no further; that therefore its extent may increase for ever, and be properly termed, indefinite or unlimited. But the fallacy and absurdity of this argument will sufficiently appear from a slight examination of what Mr. Con-

---

* Many, I doubt not, will think that the attempting gravely to controvert so absurd a paradox as the immortality of man on earth, or indeed, even the perfectibility of man and society, is a waste of time and words, and that such unfounded conjectures are best answered by neglect. I profess, however, to be of a different opinion. When paradoxes of this kind are advanced by ingenious and able men, neglect has no tendency to convince them of their mistakes. Priding themselves on what they conceive to be a mark of the reach and size of their own understandings, of the extent and comprehensiveness of their views; they will look upon this neglect merely as an indication of poverty, and narrowness, in the mental exertions of their contemporaries; and only think, that the world is not yet prepared to receive their sublime truths.

On the contrary, a candid investigation of these subjects, accompanied with a perfect readiness to adopt any theory warranted by sound philosophy, may have a tendency to convince them that in forming improbable and unfounded hypotheses, so far from enlarging the bounds of human science, they are contracting it, so far from promoting the improvement of the human mind, they are obstructing it; they are throwing us back again almost into the infancy of knowledge and weakening the foundations of that mode of philosophising, under the auspices of which, science has of late made such rapid advances. The present rage for wide and unrestrained speculation seems to be a kind of mental intoxication, arising, perhaps, from the great and unexpected discoveries which have been made of late years, in various branches of science. To men elate and giddy with such successes, every thing appeared to be within the grasp of human powers; and, under this illusion, they confounded subjects where no real progress could be proved, with those, where the progress had been marked, certain, and acknowledged. Could they be persuaded to sober themselves with a little severe and chastized thinking, they would see, that the cause of truth, and of sound philosophy, cannot but suffer by substituting wild flights and unsupported assertions, for patient investigation, and well authenticated proofs.

dorcet calls the organic perfectibility, or degeneration, of the race
of plants and animals, which he says may be regarded as one of
the general laws of nature.

I am told that it is a maxim among the improvers of cattle that
you may breed to any degree of nicety you please, and they found
this maxim upon another, which is that some of the offspring will
possess the desirable qualities of the parents in a greater degree.
In the famous Leicestershire breed of sheep, the object is to procure
them with small heads and small legs. Proceeding upon these
breeding maxims, it is evident that we might go on till the heads
and legs were evanescent quantities, but this is so palpable an
absurdity that we may be quite sure that the premises are not just
and that there really is a limit, though we cannot see it or say
exactly where it is. In this case, the point of the greatest degree of
improvement, or the smallest size of the head and legs, may be
said to be undefined, but this is very different from unlimited, or
from indefinite, in Mr. Condorcet's acceptation of the term.
Though I may not be able in the present instance to mark the
limit at which further improvement will stop, I can very easily
mention a point at which it will not arrive. I should not scruple
to assert that were the breeding to continue for ever, the head and
legs of these sheep would never be so small as the head and legs
of a rat.

It cannot be true, therefore, that among animals, some of the
offspring will possess the desirable qualities of the parents in a
greater degree, or that animals are indefinitely perfectible.

The progress of a wild plant to a beautiful garden flower is
perhaps more marked and striking than any thing that takes place
among animals, yet even here it would be the height of absurdity
to assert that the progress was unlimited or indefinite. One of the
most obvious features of the improvement is the increase of size.
The flower has grown gradually larger by cultivation. If the
progress were really unlimited it might be increased ad infinitum,
but this is so gross an absurdity that we may be quite sure that
among plants as well as among animals there is a limit to improvement, though we do not exactly know where it is. It is probable
that the gardeners who contend for flower prizes have often applied
stronger dressing without success. At the same time, it would be

highly presumptuous in any man to say, that he had seen the finest carnation or anemone that could ever be made to grow. He might however assert without the smallest chance of being contradicted by a future fact, that no carnation or anemone could ever by cultivation be increased to the size of a large cabbage; and yet there are assignable quantities much greater than a cabbage. No man can say that he has seen the largest ear of wheat, or the largest oak that could ever grow; but he might easily, and with perfect certainty, name a point of magnitude, at which they would not arrive. In all these cases therefore, a careful distinction should be made, between an unlimited progress, and a progress where the limit is merely undefined.

It will be said, perhaps, that the reason why plants and animals cannot increase indefinitely in size, is, that they would fall by their own weight. I answer, how do we know this but from experience? from experience of the degree of strength with which these bodies are formed. I know that a carnation, long before it reached the size of a cabbage, would not be supported by its stalk, but I only know this from my experience of the weakness and want of tenacity in the materials of a carnation stalk. There are many substances in nature of the same size that would support as large a head as a cabbage.

The reasons of the mortality of plants are at present perfectly unknown to us. No man can say why such a plant is annual, another biennial, and another endures for ages. The whole affair in all these cases, in plants, animals, and in the human race, is an affair of experience, and I only conclude that man is mortal because the invariable experience of all ages has proved the mortality of those materials of which his visible body is made.

What can we reason but from what we know.

Sound philosophy will not authorize me to alter this opinion of the mortality of man on earth, till it can be clearly proved that the human race has made, and is making, a decided progress towards an illimitable extent of life. And the chief reason why I adduced the two particular instances from animals and plants was to expose and illustrate, if I could, the fallacy of that argument which infers an unlimited progress, merely because some partial improvement has taken place, and that the limit of this improvement cannot be precisely ascertained.

The capacity of improvement in plants and animals, to a certain degree, no person can possibly doubt. A clear and decided progress has already been made, and yet, I think it appears that it would be highly absurd to say that this progress has no limits. In human life, though there are great variations from different causes, it may be doubted whether, since the world began, any organic improvement whatever in the human frame can be clearly ascertained. The foundations therefore, on which the arguments for the organic perfectibility of man rest, are unusually weak, and can only be considered, as mere conjectures. It does not, however, by any means, seem impossible, that by an attention to breed, a certain degree of improvement, similar to that among animals, might take place among men. Whether intellect could be communicated may be a matter of doubt: but size, strength, beauty, complexion, and perhaps even longevity are in a degree transmissible. The error does not seem to lie, in supposing a small degree of improvement possible, but in not discriminating between a small improvement, the limit of which is undefined, and an improvement really unlimited. As the human race however could not be improved in this way, without condemning all the bad specimens to celibacy, it is not probable, that an attention to breed should ever become general; indeed, I know of no well-directed attempts of this kind, except in the ancient family of the Bickerstaffs, who are said to have been very successful in whitening the skins, and increasing the height of their race by prudent marriages, particularly by that very judicious cross with Maud, the milk-maid, by which some capital defects in the constitutions of the family were corrected.

It will not be necessary, I think, in order more completely to shew the improbability of any approach in man towards immortality on earth, to urge the very great additional weight that an increase in the duration of life would give to the argument of population.

Mr. Condorcet's book may be considered, not only as a sketch of the opinions of a celebrated individual, but of many of the literary men in France at the beginning of the revolution. As such, though merely a sketch, it seems worthy of attention.

CHAPTER X

In reading Mr. Godwin's ingenious and able work on political justice, it is impossible not to be struck with the spirit and energy of his style, the force and precision of some of his reasonings, the ardent tone of his thoughts, and particularly with that impressive earnestness of manner which gives an air of truth to the whole. At the same time, it must be confessed that he has not proceeded in his enquiries with the caution that sound philosophy seems to require. His conclusions are often unwarranted by his premises. He fails sometimes in removing the objections which he himself brings forward. He relies too much on general and abstract propositions which will not admit of application. And his conjectures certainly far outstrip the modesty of nature.

The system of equality which Mr. Godwin proposes is, without doubt, by far the most beautiful and engaging of any that has yet appeared. An amelioration of society to be produced merely by reason and conviction wears much more the promise of permanence, than any change effected and maintained by force. The unlimited exercise of private judgment is a doctrine inexpressibly grand and captivating and has a vast superiority over those systems where every individual is in a manner the slave of the public. The substitution of benevolence as the master-spring and moving principle of society, instead of self-love, is a consummation devoutly to be wished. In short, it is impossible to contemplate the whole of this fair structure, without emotions of delight and admiration, accompanied with ardent longing for the period of its accomplishment. But, alas! that moment can never arrive. The whole is little better than a dream, a beautiful phantom of the imagination. These "gorgeous palaces" of happiness and immortality, these "solemn temples" of truth and virtue will dissolve, "like the baseless fabric of a vision," when we awaken to real life and contemplate the true and genuine situation of man on earth.

Mr. Godwin, at the conclusion of the third chapter of his eighth book, speaking of population, says, "There is a principle in human society, by which population is perpetually kept down to the level of the means of subsistence. Thus among the wandering tribes of America and Asia, we never find through the lapse of ages that population has so increased as to render necessary the cultivation of the earth." This principle, which Mr. Godwin thus mentions as some mysterious and occult cause and which he does not attempt to investigate, will be found to be the grinding law of necessity, misery, and the fear of misery.

The great error under which Mr. Godwin labours throughout his whole work is the attributing almost all the vices and misery that are seen in civil society to human institutions. Political regulations and the established administration of property are with him the fruitful sources of all evil, the hotbeds of all the crimes that degrade mankind. Were this really a true state of the case, it would not seem a hopeless task to remove evil completely from the world, and reason seems to be the proper and adequate instrument for effecting so great a purpose. But the truth is, that though human institutions appear to be the obvious and obtrusive causes of much mischief to mankind, yet, in reality they are light and superficial, they are mere feathers that float on the surface, in comparison with those deeper seated causes of impurity that corrupt the springs and render turbid the whole stream of human life.

Mr. Godwin, in his chapter on the benefits attendant on a system of equality, says, "The spirit of oppression, the spirit of servility, and the spirit of fraud, these are the immediate growth of the established administration of property. They are alike hostile to intellectual improvement. The other vices of envy, malice, and revenge are their inseparable companions. In a state of society where men lived in the midst of plenty and where all shared alike the bounties of nature, these sentiments would inevitably expire. The narrow principle of selfishness would vanish. No man being obliged to guard his little store or provide with anxiety and pain for his restless wants, each would lose his individual existence in the thought of the general good. No man would be an enemy to his neighbour, for they would have no subject of contention, and, of consequence, philanthropy would resume the empire which reason assigns her. Mind would be delivered from her perpetual anxiety about corporal support, and free to expatiate in the field of thought, which is congenial to her. Each would assist the enquiries of all."

This would, indeed, be a happy state. But that it is merely an imaginary picture, with scarcely a feature near the truth, the reader, I am afraid, is already too well convinced.

Man cannot live in the midst of plenty. All cannot share alike the bounties of nature. Were there no established administration of property, every man would be obliged to guard with force his little store. Selfishness would be triumphant. The subjects of contention would be perpetual. Every individual mind would be under a constant anxiety about corporal support, and not a single intellect would be left free to expatiate in the field of thought.

How little Mr. Godwin has turned the attention of his penetrating mind to the real state of man on earth will sufficiently appear from the manner in which he endeavours to remove the difficulty of an overcharged population. He says, "The obvious answer to this objection, is, that to reason thus is to foresee difficulties at a great distance. Three fourths of the habitable globe is now uncultivated. The parts already cultivated are capable of immeasureable improvement. Myriads of centuries of still increasing population may pass away, and the earth be still found sufficient for the subsistence of its inhabitants."

I have already pointed out the error of supposing that no distress and difficulty would arise from an overcharged population before the earth absolutely refused to produce any more. But let us imagine for a moment Mr. Godwin's beautiful system of equality realized in its utmost purity, and see how soon this difficulty might be expected to press under so perfect a form of society. A theory that will not admit of application cannot possibly be just.

Let us suppose all the causes of misery and vice in this island removed. War and contention cease. Unwholesome trades and manufactories do not exist. Crowds no longer collect together in

great and pestilent cities for purposes of court intrigue, of commerce, and vicious gratifications. Simple, healthy, and rational
amusements take place of drinking, gaming, and debauchery.
There are no towns sufficiently large to have any prejudicial effects
on the human constitution. The greater part of the happy inhabitants of this terrestrial paradise live in hamlets and farm-houses
scattered over the face of the country. Every house is clean, airy,
sufficiently roomy, and in a healthy situation. All men are equal.
The labours of luxury are at end. And the necessary labours of
agriculture are shared amicably among all. The number of persons, and the produce of the island, we suppose to be the same as
at present. The spirit of benevolence, guided by impartial justice,
will divide this produce among all the members of the society
according to their wants. Though it would be impossible that they
should all have animal food every day, yet vegetable food, with
meat occasionally, would satisfy the desires of a frugal people and
would be sufficient to preserve them in health, strength, and spirits.

Mr. Godwin considers marriage as a fraud and a monopoly.
Let us suppose the commerce of the sexes established upon principles of the most perfect freedom. Mr. Godwin does not think
himself that this freedom would lead to a promiscuous intercourse,
and in this I perfectly agree with him. The love of variety is a
vicious, corrupt, and unnatural taste and could not prevail in any
great degree in a simple and virtuous state of society. Each man
would probably select himself a partner, to whom he would adhere
as long as that adherence continued to be the choice of both
parties. It would be of little consequence, according to Mr.
Godwin, how many children a woman had or to whom they
belonged. Provisions and assistance would spontaneously flow
from the quarter in which they abounded, to the quarter that was
deficient.* And every man would be ready to furnish instruction
to the rising generation according to his capacity.

I cannot conceive a form of society so favourable upon the
whole to population. The irremediableness of marriage, as it is at
present constituted, undoubtedly deters many from entering into
that state. An unshackled intercourse on the contrary would be a

---

* See B. 8. Chap. 8. P. 504.

most powerful incitement to early attachments, and as we are supposing no anxiety about the future support of children to exist, I do not conceive that there would be one woman in a hundred, of twenty three, without a family.

With these extraordinary encouragements to population, and every cause of depopulation, as we have supposed, removed, the numbers would necessarily increase faster than in any society that has ever yet been known. I have mentioned, on the authority of a pamphlet published by a Dr. Styles and referred to by Dr. Price, that the inhabitants of the back settlements of America doubled their numbers in fifteen years. England is certainly a more healthy country than the back settlements of America, and as we have supposed every house in the island to be airy and wholesome, and the encouragements to have a family greater even than with the back settlers, no probable reason can be assigned why the population should not double itself in less, if possible, than fifteen years. But to be quite sure that we do not go beyond the truth, we will only suppose the period of doubling to be twenty-five years, a ratio of increase, which is well known to have taken place throughout all the Northern States of America.

There can be little doubt that the equalization of property which we have supposed, added to the circumstance of the labour of the whole community being directed chiefly to agriculture, would tend greatly to augment the produce of the country. But to answer the demands of a population increasing so rapidly, Mr. Godwin's calculation of half an hour a day for each man, would certainly not be sufficient. It is probable that the half of every man's time must be employed for this purpose. Yet with such, or much greater exertions, a person who is acquainted with the nature of the soil in this country, and who reflects on the fertility of the lands already in cultivation, and the barrenness of those that are not cultivated, will be very much disposed to doubt whether the whole average produce could possibly be doubled in twenty-five years from the present period. The only chance of success would be the ploughing up all the grazing countries and putting an end almost entirely to the use of animal food. Yet a part of this scheme might defeat itself. The soil of England will not produce much without dressing, and cattle seem to be necessary to make that species of manure which best suits the land. In China it is said that the soil in some of the provinces is so fertile as to produce two crops of rice in the year without dressing. None of the lands in England will answer to this description.

Difficult, however, as it might be to double the average produce of the island in twenty-five years, let us suppose it effected. At the expiration of the first period therefore, the food, though almost entirely vegetable, would be sufficient to support in health, the doubled population of fourteen millions.

During the next period of doubling, where will the food be found to satisfy the importunate demands of the increasing numbers. Where is the fresh land to turn up? where is the dressing necessary to improve that which is already in cultivation? There is no person with the smallest knowledge of land, but would say that it was impossible that the average produce of the country could be increased during the second twenty-five years by a quantity equal to what it at present yields. Yet we will suppose this increase, however improbable, to take place. The exuberant strength of the argument allows of almost any concession. Even with this concession, however, there would be seven millions at the expiration of the second term, unprovided for. A quantity of food equal to the frugal support of twenty-one millions, would be to be divided among twenty-eight millions.

Alas! what becomes of the picture where men lived in the midst of plenty, where no man was obliged to provide with anxiety and pain for his restless wants, where the narrow principle of selfishness did not exist, where Mind was delivered from her perpetual anxiety about corporal support and free to expatiate in the field of thought which is congenial to her. This beautiful fabric of imagination vanishes at the severe touch of truth. The spirit of benevolence, cherished and invigorated by plenty, is repressed by the chilling breath of want. The hateful passions that had vanished, reappear. The mighty law of self-preservation, expels all the softer and more exalted emotions of the soul. The temptations to evil are too strong for human nature to resist. The corn is plucked before it is ripe, or secreted in unfair proportions, and the whole black train of vices that belong to falsehood are immediately generated. Provisions no longer flow in for the support of the mother with a large family. The children are sickly from insufficient food. The rosy flush of health gives place to the pallid cheek and hollow eye of misery. Benevolence yet lingering in a few bosoms, makes some faint expiring struggles, till at length self-love resumes his wonted empire and lords it triumphant over the world.

No human institutions here existed, to the perverseness of which Mr. Godwin ascribes the original sin of the worst men.* No opposition had been produced by them between public and private good. No monopoly had been created of those advantages which reason directs to be left in common. No man had been goaded to the breach of order by unjust laws. Benevolence had established her reign in all hearts: and yet in so short a period as within fifty years, violence, oppression, falsehood, misery, every hateful vice, and every form of distress, which degrade and sadden the present state of society, seem to have been generated by the most imperious circumstances, by laws inherent in the nature of man, and absolutely independent of all human regulations.

If we are not yet too well convinced of the reality of this melancholy picture, let us but look for a moment into the next period of twenty-five years; and we shall see twenty-eight millions of human beings without the means of support; and before the conclusion of the first century, the population would be one hundred and twelve millions, and the food only sufficient for thirty-five millions, leaving seventy-seven millions unprovided for. In these ages want would be indeed triumphant, and rapine and murder must reign at large: and yet all this time we are supposing the produce of the earth absolutely unlimited, and the yearly increase greater than the boldest speculator can imagine.

This is undoubtedly a very different view of the difficulty arising from population, from that which Mr. Godwin gives, when he says, "Myriads of centuries of still increasing population may pass away, and the earth be still found sufficient for the subsistence of its inhabitants."

I am sufficiently aware that the redundant twenty-eight millions, or seventy-seven millions, that I have mentioned, could never have existed. It is a perfectly just observation of Mr. Godwin, that,

---

* B. 8. C. 3. P. 340.

"There is a principle in human society, by which population is perpetually kept down to the level of the means of subsistence." The sole question is, what is this princeple? It is some obscure and occult cause? Is it some mysterious interference of heaven, which at a certain period, strikes the men with impotence, and the women with barrenness? Or is it a cause, open to our researches, within our view, a cause, which has constantly been observed to operate, though with varied force, in every state in which man has been placed? Is it not a degree of misery, the necessary and inevitable result of the laws of nature, which human institutions, so far from aggravating, have tended considerably to mitigate, though they never can remove?

It may be curious to observe, in the case that we have been supposing, how some of the laws which at present govern civilized society, would be successively dictated by the most imperious necessity. As man, according to Mr. Godwin, is the creature of the impressions to which he is subject, the goadings of want could not continue long, before some violations of public or private stock would necessarily take place. As these violations increased in number and extent, the more active and comprehensive intellects of the society would soon perceive, that while population was fast increasing, the yearly produce of the country would shortly begin to diminish. The urgency of the case would suggest the necessity of some immediate measures to be taken for the general safety. Some kind of convention would then be called, and the dangerous situation of the country stated in the strongest terms. It would be observed, that while they lived in the midst of plenty, it was of little consequence who laboured the least, or who possessed the least, as every man was perfectly willing and ready to supply the wants of his neighbour. But that the question was no longer, whether one man should give to another, that which he did not use himself; but whether he should give to his neighbour the food which was absolutely necessary to his own existence. It would be represented, that the number of those that were in want very greatly exceeded the number and means of those who should supply them: that these pressing wants, which from the state of the produce of the country could not all be gratified, had occasioned some flagrant violations of justice: that these violations had already checked the increase

of food, and would, if they were not by some means or other prevented, throw the whole community in confusion: that imperious
necessity seemed to dictate that a yearly increase of produce
should, if possible, be obtained at all events: that in order to effect this first, great, and indispensible purpose, it would be adviseable to make a more complete division of land, and to secure every
man's stock against violation by the most powerful sanctions, even
by death itself.

It might be urged perhaps by some objectors, that, as the fertility
of the land increased, and various accidents occurred, the share of
some men might be much more than sufficient for their support,
and that when the reign of self-love was once established, they
would not distribute their surplus produce without some com-
pensation in return. It would be observed, in answer, that this was
an inconvenience greatly to be lamented; but that it was an evil
which bore no comparison to the black train of distresses, that
would inevitably be occasioned by the insecurity of property: that
the quantity of food which one man could consume, was necessarily limited by the narrow capacity of the human stomach: that
it was not certainly probable that he should throw away the rest;
but that even if he exchanged his surplus food for the labour of
others, and made them in some degree dependent on him, this
would still be better than that these others should absolutely
starve.

It seems highly probable, therefore, that an administration of
property, not very different from that which prevails in civilized
States at present, would be established, as the best, though inadequate, remedy, for the evils which were pressing on the society.

The next subject that would come under discussion, intimately
connected with the preceding, is, the commerce between the sexes.
It would be urged by those who had turned their attention to the
true cause of the difficulties under which the community laboured,
that while every man felt secure that all his children would be well
provided for by general benevolence, the powers of the earth
would be absolutely inadequate to produce food for the population which would inevitably ensue: that even, if the whole attention and labour of the society were directed to this sole point, and
if, by the most perfect security of property, and every other encour-

agement that could be thought of, the greatest possible increase of
produce were yearly obtained; yet still, that the increase of food
would by no means keep pace with the much more rapid increase
of population: that some check to population therefore was im-
periously called for: that the most natural and obvious check
seemed to be, to make every man provide for his own children:
that this would operate in some respect, as a measure and guide,
in the increase of population; as it might be expected that no man
would bring beings into the world, for whom he could not find
the means of support: that where this notwithstanding was the
case, it seemed necessary, for the example of others, that the disgrace and inconvenience attending such a conduct, should fall
upon the individual, who had thus inconsiderately plunged himself and innocent children in misery and want.

The institution of marriage, or at least, of some express or
implied obligation on every man to support his own children,
seems to be the natural result of these reasonings in a community
under the difficulties that we have supposed.

The view of these difficulties, presents us with a very natural
origin of the superior disgrace which attends a breach of chastity
in the woman, than in the man. It could not be expected that
women should have resources sufficient to support their own
children. When therefore a woman was connected with a man,
who had entered into no compact to maintain her children; and
aware of the inconveniences that he might bring upon himself,
had deserted her, these children must necessarily fall for support
upon the society, or starve. And to prevent the frequent recurrence
of such an inconvenience, as it would be highly unjust to punish
so natural a fault by personal restraint or infliction, the men
might agree to punish it with disgrace. The offence is besides more
obvious and conspicuous in the woman, and less liable to any
mistake. The father of a child may not always be known, but the
same uncertainty cannot easily exist with regard to the mother.
Where the evidence of the offence was most complete, and the
inconvenience to the society at the same time the greatest, there,
it was agreed, that the largest share of blame should fall. The obligation on every man to maintain his children, the society would
enforce, if there were occasion; and the greater degree of inconven-

ience or labour, to which a family would necessarily subject him, added to some portion of disgrace which every human being must incur, who leads another into unhappiness, might be considered as a sufficient punishment for the man.

That a woman should at present be almost driven from society, for an offence, which men commit nearly with impunity, seems to be undoubtedly a breach of natural justice. But the origin of the custom, as the most obvious and effectual method of preventing the frequent recurrence of a serious inconvenience to a community, appears to be natural, though not perhaps perfectly justifiable. This origin, however, is now lost in the new train of ideas which the custom has since generated. What at first might be dictated by state necessity, is now supported by female delicacy; and operates with the greatest force on that part of society, where, if the original intention of the custom were preserved, there is the least real occasion for it.

When these two fundamental laws of society, the security of property, and the institution of marriage, were once established, inequality of conditions must necessarily follow. Those who were born after the division of property, would come into a world already possessed. If their parents, from having too large a family, could not give them sufficient for their support, what are they to do in a world where every thing is appropriated? We have seen the fatal effects that would result to a society, if every man had a valid claim to an equal share of the produce of the earth. The members of a family which was grown too large for the original division of land appropriated to it, could not then demand a part of the surplus produce of others, as a debt of justice. It has appeared, that from the inevitable laws of our nature, some human beings must suffer from want. These are the unhappy persons who, in the great lottery of life, have drawn a blank. The number of these claimants would soon exceed the ability of the surplus produce to supply. Moral merit is a very difficult distinguishing criterion, except in extreme cases. The owners of surplus produce would in general seek some more obvious mark of distinction. And it seems both natural and just, that except upon particular occasions, their choice should fall upon those, who were able, and professed themselves willing, to exert their strength in procuring a further surplus produce; and thus at once benefitting the community, and enabling these proprietors to afford assistance to greater numbers. All who were in want of food would be urged by imperious necessity to offer their labour in exchange for this article so absolutely essential to existence. The fund appropriated to the maintenance of labour, would be, the aggregate quantity of food possessed by the owners of land beyond their own consumption. When the demands upon this fund were great and numerous, it would naturally be divided in very small shares. Labour would be ill paid. Men would offer to work for a bare subsistence, and the rearing of families would be checked by sickness and misery. On the contrary, when this fund was increasing fast; when it was great in proportion to the number of claimants; it would be divided in much larger shares. No man would exchange his labour without receiving an ample quantity of food in return. Labourers would live in ease and comfort; and would consequently be able to rear a numerous and vigorous offspring.

On the state of this fund, the happiness, or the degree of misery, prevailing among the lower classes of people in every known State, at present chiefly depends. And on this happiness, or degree of misery, depends the increase, stationariness, or decrease of population.

And thus it appears, that a society constituted according to the most beautiful form that imagination can conceive, with benevolence for its moving principle, instead of self-love, and with every evil disposition in all its members corrected by reason and not force, would, from the inevitable laws of nature, and not from any original depravity of man, in a very short period, degenerate into a society, constructed upon a plan not essentially different from that which prevails in every known State at present; I mean, a society divided into a class of proprietors, and a class of labourers, and with self-love the main-spring of the great machine.

In the supposition I have made, I have undoubtedly taken the increase of population smaller, and the increase of produce greater, than they really would be. No reason can be assigned, why, under the circumstances I have supposed, population should not increase faster than in any known instance. If then we were to take the period of doubling at fifteen years, instead of twenty-five years; and reflect upon the labour necessary to double the produce in so short a time, even if we allow it possible; we may venture to pronounce with certainty, that if Mr. Godwin's system of society was established in its utmost perfection, instead of myriads of centuries, not thirty years could elapse, before its utter destruction from the simple principle of population.

I have taken no notice of emigration for obvious reasons. If such societies were instituted in other parts of Europe, these countries would be under the same difficulties with regard to population, and could admit no fresh members into their bosoms. If this beautiful society were confined to this island, it must have degenerated strangely from its original purity, and administer but a very small portion of the happiness it proposed; in short, its essential principle must be completely destroyed, before any of its members would voluntarily consent to leave it, and live under such governments as at present exist in Europe, or submit to the extreme hardships of first settlers in new regions. We well know, from repeated experience, how much misery and hardship men will undergo in their own country, before they can determine to desert it; and how often the most tempting proposals of embarking for new settlements have been rejected by people who appeared to be almost starving.

CHAPTER XI

We have supposed Mr. Godwin's system of society once completely established. But it is supposing an impossibility. The same causes in nature which would destroy it so rapidly, were it once established, would prevent the possibility of its establishment. And upon what grounds we can presume a change in these natural causes, I am utterly at a loss to conjecture. No move towards the extinction of the passion between the sexes has taken place in the five or six thousand years that the world has existed. Men in the decline of life have in all ages declaimed a passion which they have ceased to feel, but with as little reason as success. Those who from coldness of constitutional temperament have never felt what love is, will surely be allowed to be very incompetent judges with regard to the power of this passion to contribute to the sum of pleasurable sensations in life. Those who have spent their youth in criminal excesses and have prepared for themselves, as the comforts of their age corporal debility and mental remorse may well inveigh against such pleasures as vain and futile, and unproductive of lasting satisfaction. But the pleasures of pure love will bear the contemplation of the most improved reason, and the most exalted virtue. Perhaps there is scarcely a man who has once experienced the genuine delight of virtuous love, however great his intellectual pleasures may have been, that does not look back to the period as the sunny spot in his whole life, where his imagination loves to bask, which he recollects and contemplates with the fondest regrets, and which he would most wish to live over again. The superiority of intellectual to sensual pleasures consists rather in their filling up more time, in their having a larger range, and in their being less liable to satiety, than in their being more real and essential.

Intemperance in every enjoyment defeats its own purpose. A walk in the finest day through the most beautiful country, if pursued too far, ends in pain and fatigue. The most wholesome and invigorating food, eaten with an unrestrained appetite, produces weakness instead of strength. Even intellectual pleasures, though certainly less liable than others to satiety, pursued with too little intermission, debilitate the body, and impair the vigour of the mind. To argue against the reality of these pleasures from their abuse seems to be hardly just. Morality, according to Mr. Godwin, is a calculation of consequences, or, as Archdeacon Paley very justly expresses it, the will of God, as collected from general expediency. According to either of these definitions, a sensual pleasure not attended with the probability of unhappy consequences does not offend against the laws of morality, and if it be pursued with such a degree of temperance, as to leave the most ample room for intellectual attainments, it must undoubtedly add to the sum of pleasurable sensations in life. Virtuous love, exalted by friendship, seems to be that sort of mixture of sensual and intellectual enjoyment particularly suited to the nature of man, and most powerfully calculated to awaken the sympathies of the soul, and produce the most exquisite gratifications.

Mr. Godwin says, in order to shew the evident inferiority of the pleasures of sense, "Strip the commerce of the sexes of all its attendant circumstances,* and it would be generally despised." He might as well say to a man who admired trees: strip them of their spreading branches and lovely foliage, and what beauty can you see in a bare pole? But it was the tree with the branches and foliage, and not without them, that excited admiration. One feature of an object, may be as distinct, and excite as different emotions, from the aggregate, as any two things the most remote, as a beautiful woman, and a map of Madagascar. It is "the symmetry of person, the vivacity, the voluptuous softness of temper, the affectionate kindness of feelings, the imagination and the wit" of a woman that excite the passion of love, and not the mere distinction of her being a female. Urged by the passion of love, men have been driven into acts highly prejudicial to the general interests of

---

* B. 1. C. 5. P. 73.

society, but probably they would have found no difficulty in resisting the temptation, had it appeared in the form of a woman with no other attractions whatever but her sex. To strip sensual pleasures of all their adjuncts, in order to prove their inferiority, is to deprive a magnet of some of its most essential causes of attraction, and then to say that it is weak and inefficient.

In the pursuit of every enjoyment, whether sensual or intellectual, Reason, that faculty which enables us to calculate consequences, is the proper corrective and guide. It is probable therefore that improved reason will always tend to prevent the abuse of sensual pleasures, though it by no means follows that it will extinguish them.

I have endeavored to expose the fallacy of that argument which infers an unlimited progress from a partial improvement, the limits of which cannot be exactly ascertained. It has appeared, I think, that there are many instances in which a decided progress has been observed, where yet it would be a gross absurdity to suppose that progress indefinite. But towards the extinction of the passion between the sexes, no observable progress whatever has hitherto been made. To suppose such an extinction, therefore, is merely to offer an unfounded conjecture, unsupported by any philosophical probabilities.

It is a truth, which history I am afraid makes too clear, that some men of the highest mental powers, have been addicted not only to a moderate, but even to an immoderate indulgence in the pleasures of sensual love. But allowing, as I should be inclined to do, notwithstanding numerous instances to the contrary, that great intellectual exertions tend to diminish the empire of this passion over man, it is evident that the mass of mankind must be improved more highly than the brightest ornaments of the species at present before any difference can take place sufficient sensibly to affect population. I would by no means suppose that the mass of mankind has reached its term of improvement, but the principal argument of this essay tends to place in a strong point of view, the improbability, that the lower classes of people in any country, should ever be sufficiently free from want and labour, to obtain any high degree of intellectual improvement.

CHAPTER XII

Mr. Godwin's conjecture respecting the future approach of man towards immortality on earth seems to be rather oddly placed in a chapter which professes to remove the objection to his system of equality from the principle of population. Unless he supposes the passion between the sexes to decrease faster than the duration of life increases, the earth would be more encumbered than ever. But leaving this difficulty to Mr. Godwin, let us examine a few of the appearances from which the probable immortality of man is inferred.

To prove the power of the mind over the body, Mr. Godwin observes, "How often do we find a piece of good news dissipating a distemper? How common is the remark that those accidents which are to the indolent a source of disease are forgotten and extirpated in the busy and active? I walk twenty miles in an indolent and half determined temper and am extremely fatigued. I walk twenty miles full of ardour, and with a motive that engrosses my soul, and I come in as fresh and as alert as when I began my journey. Emotions excited by some unexpected word, by a letter that is delivered to us, occasions the most extraordinary revolutions in our frame, accelerates the circulation, causes the heart to palpitate, the tongue to refuse its office, and has been known to occasion death by extreme anguish or extreme joy. There is nothing indeed of which the physician is more aware than of the power of the mind in assisting or retarding convalescence."

The instances here mentioned, are chiefly instances of the effects of mental stimulants on the bodily frame. No person has ever for a moment doubted the near, though mysterious connection, of mind and body. But it is arguing totally without knowledge of the nature of stimulants to suppose, either that they can be applied continually with equal strength, or if they could be so applied, for a time, that they would not exhaust and wear out the subject. In some of the cases here noticed, the strength of the stimulus depends upon its novelty and unexpectedness. Such a stimulus cannot, from its nature, be repeated often with the same effect, as it would by repetition lose that property which gives it its strength.

In the other cases, the argument is from a small and partial effect, to a great and general effect, which will in numberless instances be found to be a very fallacious mode of reasoning. The busy and active man may in some degree counteract, or what is perhaps nearer the truth, may disregard those slight disorders of frame, which fix the attention of a man who has nothing else to think of; but this does not tend to prove that activity of mind will enable a man to disregard a high fever, the smallpox, or the plague.

The man who walks twenty miles with a motive that engrosses his soul, does not attend to his slight fatigue of body when he comes in; but double his motive, and set him to walk another twenty miles, quadruple it, and let him start a third time, and so on; and the length of his walk will ultimately depend upon muscle and not mind. Powel, for a motive of ten guineas, would have walked further probably than Mr. Godwin, for a motive of half a million. A motive of uncommon power acting upon a frame of moderate strength, would, perhaps, make the man kill himself by his exertions, but it would not make him walk an hundred miles in twenty-four hours. This statement of the case, shews the fallacy of supposing, that the person was really not at all tired in his first walk of twenty miles, because he did not appear to be so, or, perhaps, scarcely felt any fatigue himself. The mind cannot fix its attention strongly on more than one object at once. The twenty thousand pounds so engrossed his thoughts, that he did not attend to any slight soreness of foot, or stiffness of limb. But had he been really as fresh and as alert, as when he first set off, he would be able to go the second twenty miles with as much ease as the first, and so on, the third, &c. which leads to a palpable absurdity. When a horse of spirit is nearly half tired, by the stimulus of the spur, added to the proper management of the bit, he may be put so much upon his mettle, that he would appear to a stander-by, as fresh and as high spirited, as if he had not gone a mile. Nay, probably, the horse himself, while in the heat and passion occasioned by this stimulus, would not feel any fatigue; but it would be strangely contrary to all reason and experience, to argue from such an appearance, that if the stimulus were continued, the horse would never be tired. The cry of a pack of hounds will make some horses, after a journey of forty miles on the road, appear as fresh, and as lively, as when they first set out. Were they then to be hunted, no perceptible abatement would at first be felt by their riders in their strength and spirits, but towards the end of a hard day, the previous fatigue would have its full weight and effect, and make them tire sooner. When I have taken a long walk with my gun, and met with no success, I have frequently returned home feeling a considerable degree of uncomfortableness from fatigue. Another day, perhaps, going over nearly the same extent of ground with a good deal of sport, I have come home fresh, and alert. The difference in the sensation of fatigue upon coming in, on the different days, may have been very striking, but on the following mornings I have found no such difference. I have not perceived that I was less stiff in my limbs, or less footsore, on the morning after the day of the sport, than on the other morning.

In all these cases, stimulants upon the mind seem to act rather by taking off the attention from the bodily fatigue, than by really and truly counteracting it. If the energy of my mind had really counteracted the fatigue of my body, why should I feel tired the next morning? If the stimulus of the hounds had as completely overcome the fatigue of the journey in reality, as it did in appearance, why should the horse be tired sooner than if he had not gone the forty miles? I happen to have a very bad fit of the tooth-ache at the time I am writing this. In the eagerness of composition, I every now and then, for a moment or two, forget it. Yet I cannot help thinking that the process which causes the pain, is still going forwards, and that the nerves which carry the information of it to the brain are even during these moments demanding attention and room for their appropriate vibrations. The multiplicity of vibrations of another kind may perhaps prevent their admission, or overcome them for a time when admitted, till a shoot of extraordinary energy puts all other vibrations to the rout, destroys the vividness of my argumentative conceptions, and rides triumphant in the brain. In this case, as in the others, the mind seems to have little or no power in counteracting, or curing the disorder, but merely possesses a power, if strongly excited, of fixing its attention on other subjects.

I do not, however, mean to say that a sound and vigorous mind has no tendency whatever to keep the body in a similar state. So close and intimate is the union of mind and body that it would be highly extraordinary if they did not mutually assist each other's functions. But, perhaps, upon a comparison, the body has more effect upon the mind, than the mind upon the body. The first object of the mind is to act as purveyor to the wants of the body. When these wants are completely satisfied, an active mind is indeed apt to wander further, to range over the fields of science, or sport in the regions of imagination, to fancy that it has "shuffled off this mortal coil," and is seeking its kindred element. But all these efforts are like the vain exertions of the hare in the fable. The slowly moving tortoise, the body, never fails to overtake the mind, however widely and extensively it may have ranged, and the brightest and most energetic intellects, unwillingly as they may attend to the first or second summons, must ultimately yield the empire of the brain to the calls of hunger, or sink with the exhausted body in sleep.

It seems as if one might say with certainty that if a medicine could be found to immortalize the body there would be no fear of its being accompanied by the immortality of the mind. But the immortality of the mind by no means seems to infer the immortality of the body. On the contrary, the greatest conceivable energy of mind would probably exhaust and destroy the strength of the body. A temperate vigour of mind appears to be favourable to health, but very great intellectual exertions tend rather, as has been often observed, to wear out the scabbard. Most of the instances which Mr. Godwin has brought to prove the power of the mind over the body, and the consequent probability of the immortality of man, are of this latter description, and could such stimulants be continually applied, instead of tending to immortalize, they would tend very rapidly to destroy the human frame.

The probable increase of the voluntary power of man over his animal frame comes next under Mr. Godwin's consideration, and he concludes by saying, that the voluntary power of some men, in this respect, is found to extend to various articles in which other men are impotent. But this is reasoning against an almost universal rule from a few exceptions; and these exceptions seem to be rather tricks, than powers that may be exerted to any good purpose. I have never heard of any man who could regulate his pulse in a fever, and doubt much, if any of the persons here alluded to have made the smallest perceptible progress in the regular correction of the disorders of their frames and the consequent prolongation of their lives.

Mr. Godwin says, "Nothing can be more unphilosophical than to conclude, that, because a certain species of power is beyond the train of our present observation, that it is beyond the limits of the human mind." I own my ideas of philosophy are in this respect widely different from Mr. Godwin's. The only distinction that I see, between a philosophical conjecture, and the assertions of the Prophet Mr. Brothers, is, that one is founded upon indications arising from the train of our present observations, and the other has no foundation at all. I expect that great discoveries are yet to take place in all the branches of human science, particularly in physics; but the moment we leave past experience as the foundation of our conjectures concerning the future; and still more, if our conjectures absolutely contradict past experience, we are thrown upon a wide field of uncertainty, and any one supposition is then just as good as another. If a person were to tell me that men would ultimately have eyes and hands behind them as well as before them, I should admit the usefulness of the addition, but should give as a reason for my disbelief of it, that I saw no indications whatever in the past from which I could infer the smallest probability of such a change. If this be not allowed a valid objection, all conjectures are alike, and all equally philosophical. I own it appears to me that in the train of our present observations, there are no more genuine indications that man will become immortal upon earth, than that he will have four eyes and four hands, or that trees will grow horizontally instead of perpendicularly.

It will be said, perhaps, that many discoveries have already taken place in the world that were totally unforeseen and unexpected. This I grant to be true; but if a person had predicted these discoveries without being guided by any analogies or indications from past facts, he would deserve the name of seer or prophet, but not of philosopher. The wonder that some of our modern discoveries would excite in the savage inhabitants of Europe in the times of Theseus and Achilles, proves but little. Persons almost entirely unacquainted with the powers of a machine, cannot be expected to guess at its effects. I am far from saying, that we are at present by any means fully acquainted with the powers of the human mind; but we certainly know more of this instrument than was known four thousand years ago; and therefore, though not to be called competent judges, we are certainly much better able, than savages, to say what is, or is not, within its grasp. A watch would strike a Savage with as much surprize as a perpetual motion; yet one, is to us a most familiar piece of mechanism, and the other, has constantly eluded the efforts of the most acute intellects. In many instances, we are now able to perceive the causes, which prevent an unlimited improvement in those inventions, which seemed to promise fairly for it at first. The original improvers of telescopes would probably think, that as long as the size of the specula, and the length of the tubes could be increased, the powers and advantages of the instrument would increase; but experience has since taught us, that the smallness of the field, the deficiency of light, and the circumstance of the atmosphere being magnified, prevent the beneficial results that were to be expected from telescopes of extraordinary size and power. In many parts of knowledge, man has been almost constantly making some progress; in other parts, his efforts have been invariably baffled. The Savage would not probably be able to guess at the causes of this mighty difference. Our further experience has given us some little insight into these causes, and has therefore enabled us better to judge, if not, of what we are to expect in future, at least, of what we are not to expect, which, though negative, is a very useful piece of information.

As the necessity of sleep seems rather to depend upon the body than the mind, it does not appear how the improvement of the mind can tend very greatly to supersede this "conspicuous infirmity." A man who by great excitements on his mind is able to pass two or three nights without sleep, proportionably exhausts the vigour of his body, and this diminution of health and strength will soon disturb the operations of his understanding, so that by these great efforts he appears to have made no real progress whatever in superseding the necessity of this species of rest.

There is certainly a sufficiently marked difference in the various characters of which we have some knowledge, relative to the energies of their minds, their benevolent pursuits, &c. to enable us to judge, whether the operations of intellect have any decided effect in prolonging the duration of human life. It is certain that no decided effect of this kind has yet been observed. Though no attention of any kind has ever produced such an effect, as could be construed into the smallest semblance of an approach towards immortality, yet of the two, a certain attention to the body seems to have more effect in this respect than an attention to the mind. The man who takes his temperate meals, and his bodily exercise, with scrupulous regularity, will generally be found more healthy than the man who, very deeply engaged in intellectual pursuits, often forgets for a time these bodily cravings. The citizen who has retired, and whose ideas, perhaps, scarcely soar above or extend beyond his little garden, pudling all the morning about his borders of box ,will, perhaps, live as long as the philosopher whose range of intellect is the most extensive, and whose views are the clearest of any of his contemporaries. It has been positively observed by those who have attended to the bills of mortality that women live longer upon an average than men, and, though I would not by any means say that their intellectual faculties are inferior, yet, I think, it must be allowed that from their different education, there are not so many women as men, who are excited to vigorous mental exertion.

As in these and similar instances, or to take a larger range, as in the great diversity of characters that have existed during some thousand years, no decided difference has been observed in the duration of human life from the operation of intellect, the mortality of man on earth seems to be as completely established, and exactly upon the same grounds, as any one, the most constant of the laws of nature. An immediate act of power in the Creator of the Universe might, indeed, change one or all of these laws, either suddenly or gradually, but without some indications of such a

change, and such indications do not exist, it is just as unphilosophical to suppose that the life of man may be prolonged beyond
any assignable limits, as to suppose that the attraction of the earth
will gradually be changed into repulsion and that stones will
ultimately rise instead of fall or that the earth will fly off at a
certain period to some more genial and warmer sun.

The conclusion of this chapter presents us, undoubtedly, with a
very beautiful and desireable picture, but from fancy and not
imagined with truth, it fails of that interest in the heart which
nature and probability can alone give.

I cannot quit this subject without taking notice of these conjectures of Mr. Godwin and Mr. Condorcet concerning the indefinite
prolongation of human life, as a very curious instance of the longing of the soul after immortality. Both these gentlemen have
rejected the light of revelation which absolutely promises eternal
life in another state. They have also rejected the light of natural
religion, which to the ablest intellects in all ages, has indicated
the future existence of the soul. Yet so congenial is the idea of
immortality to the mind of man that they cannot consent entirely
to throw it out of their systems. After all their fastidious scepti-
cisms concerning the only probable mode of immortality, they
introduce a species of immortality of their own, not only completely contradictory to every law of philosophical probability,
but in itself in the highest degree, narrow, partial, and unjust.
They suppose that all the great, virtuous, and exalted minds, that
have ever existed or that may exist for some thousands, perhaps
millions of years, will be sunk in annihilation, and that only a few
beings, not greater in number than can exist at once upon the
earth, will be ultimately crowned with immortality. Had such a
tenet been advanced as a tenet of revelation I am very sure that
all the enemies of religion, and probably Mr. Godwin, and Mr.
Condorcet among the rest, would have exhausted the whole force
of their ridicule upon it, as the most puerile, the most absurd, the
poorest, the most pitiful, the most iniquitously unjust, and, consequently, the most unworthy of the Deity that the superstitious
folly of man could invent.

What a strange and curious proof do these conjectures exhibit
of the inconsistency of scepticism! For it should be observed, that

there is a very striking and essential difference, between believing an assertion which absolutely contradicts the most uniform experience, and an assertion which contradicts nothing, but is merely beyond the power of our present observation and knowledge.* So diversified are the natural objects around us, so many instances of mighty power daily offer themselves to our view, that we may fairly presume, that there are many forms and operations of nature which we have not yet observed, or which, perhaps, we are not capable of observing with our present confined inlets of knowledge. The resurrection of a spiritual body from a natural body, does not appear in itself a more wonderful instance of power, than the germination of a blade of wheat from the grain, or of an oak from an acorn. Could we conceive an intelligent being, so placed, as to be conversant only with inanimate, or full grown objects, and never to have witnessed the process of vegetation or growth; and were another being to shew him two little pieces of matter, a grain of wheat, and an acorn, to desire him to examine them, to analize them if he pleased, and endeavour to find out their properties and essences; and then to tell him, that however trifling these little bits of matter might appear to him, that they possessed such curious powers of selection, combination, arrangement, and almost of creation, that upon being put into the ground, they would chuse, amongst all the dirt and moisture that surrounded them, those parts which best suited their purpose, that they would collect and arrange these parts with wonderful taste, judgment, and execution, and would rise up into beautiful forms, scarcely in any respect analogous to the little bits of matter which were first placed

---

* When we extend our view beyond this life, it is evident that we can have no other guides than authority, or conjecture, and perhaps, indeed, an obscure and undefined feeling. What I say here, therefore, does not appear to me in any respect to contradict what I said before, when I observed that it was unphilosophical to expect any specifick event that was not indicated by some kind of analogy in the past. In ranging beyond the bourne from which no traveller returns, we must necessarily quit this rule; but with regard to events that may be expected to happen on earth, we can seldom quit it consistently with true philosophy. Analogy has, however, as I conceive, great latitude. For instance, man has discovered many of the laws of nature: analogy seems to indicate that he will discover many more; but no analogy seems to indicate that he will discover a sixth sense, or a new species of power in the human mind, entirely beyond the train of our present observations.

in the earth. I feel very little doubt that the imaginary being which I have supposed, would hesitate more, would require better authority, and stronger proofs, before he believed these strange assertions, than if he had been told, that a being of mighty power, who had been the cause of all that he saw around him, and of that existence of which he himself was conscious, would, by a great act of power upon the death and corruption of human creatures, raise up the essence of thought in an incorporeal, or at least invisible form, to give it a happier existence in another state.

The only difference, with regard to our own apprehensions, that is not in favour of the latter assertion, is, that the first miracle* we have repeatedly seen, and the last miracle we have not seen. I admit the full weight of this prodigious difference, but surely no man can hesitate a moment in saying that, putting Revelation out of the question, the resurrection of a spiritual body from a natural body, which may be merely one among the many operations of nature which we cannot see, is an event indefinitely more probable than the immortality of man on earth, which is not only an event, of which no symptoms or indications have yet appeared, but is a positive contradiction to one of the most constant of the laws of nature that has ever come within the observation of man.

I ought perhaps again to make an apology to my readers for dwelling so long upon a conjecture which many, I know, will think too absurd and improbable to require the least discussion. But if it be as improbable and as contrary to the genuine spirit of philosophy as I own I think it is, why should it not be shewn to

---

* The powers of selection, combination, and transmutation, which every seed shews, are truely miraculous. Who can imagine that these wonderful faculties are contained in these little bits of matter? To me it appears much more philosophical to suppose that the mighty God of nature is present in full energy in all these operations. To this all powerful Being, it would be equally easy to raise an oak without an acorn as with one. The preparatory process of putting seeds into the ground, is merely ordained for the use of man, as one among the various other excitements necessary to awaken matter into mind. It is an idea that will be found, consistent equally with the natural phenomena around us, with the various events of human life, and with the successive Revelations of God to man, to suppose that the world is a mighty process for the creation and formation of mind. Many vessels will necessarily come out of this great furnace in wrong shapes. These will be broken and thrown aside as useless; while those vessels whose forms are full of truth, grace, and loveliness, will be wafted into happier situations, nearer the presence of the mighty maker.

be so in a candid examination? A conjecture, however improbable
on the first view of it, advanced by able and ingenious men, seems
at least to deserve investigation. For my own part I feel no disin-
clination whatever, to give that degree of credit to the opinion of
the probable immortality of man on earth, which the appearances
that can be brought in support of it deserve. Before we decide
upon the utter improbability of such an event, it is but fair im-
partially to examine these appearances; and from such an examination I think we may conclude, that we have rather less reason for
supposing that the life of man may be indefinitely prolonged, than
that trees may be made to grow indefinitely high, or potatoes
indefinitely large.*

----

* Though Mr. Godwin advances the idea of the indefinite prolongation of
human life, merely as a conjecture, yet as he has produced some appearances,
which in his conception favour the supposition, he must certainly intend that
these appearances should be examined and this is all that I have meant to do.

CHAPTER XIII

In the chapter which I have been examining, Mr. Godwin professes to consider the objection to his system of equality from the principle of population. It has appeared, I think clearly, that he is greatly erroneous in his statement of the distance of this difficulty, and that instead of myriads of centuries, it is really not thirty years, or even thirty days, distant from us. The supposition of the approach of man to immortality on earth is certainly not of a kind to soften the difficulty. The only argument, therefore, in the chapter which has any tendency to remove the objection is the conjecture concerning the extinction of the passion between the sexes, but as this is a mere conjecture, unsupported by the smallest shadow of proof, the force of the objection may be fairly said to remain unimpaired, and it is undoubtedly of sufficient weight of itself completely to overturn Mr. Godwin's whole system of equality. I will, however, make one or two observations on a few of the prominent parts of Mr. Godwin's reasonings which will contribute to place in a still clearer point of view the little hope that we can reasonably entertain of those vast improvements in the nature of man and of society which he holds up to our admiring gaze in his political justice.

Mr. Godwin considers man too much in the light of a being merely intellectual. This error, at least such I conceive it to be, pervades his whole work and mixes itself with all his reasonings. The voluntary actions of men may originate in their opinions, but these opinions will be very differently modified in creatures compounded of a rational faculty and corporal propensities from what they would be in beings wholly intellectual. Mr. Godwin in proving that sound reasoning and truth are capable of being adequately communicated, examines the proposition first practically, and then adds, "Such is the appearance which this proposition assumes, when examined in a loose and practical view. In strict consideration it will not admit of debate. Man is a rational being, &c.*" So far from calling this a strict consideration of the subject, I own I should call it the loosest, and most erroneous way possible, of considering it. It is the calculating the velocity of a falling body in vacuo, and persisting in it, that it would be the same through whatever resisting mediums it might fall. This was not Newton's mode of philosophizing. Very few general propositions are just in application to a particular subject. The moon is not kept in her orbit round the earth, nor the earth in her orbit round the sun, by a force that varies merely in the inverse ratio of the squares of the distances. To make the general theory just in application to the revolutions of these bodies, it was necessary to calculate accurately, the disturbing force of the sun upon the moon, and of the moon upon the earth; and till these disturbing forces were properly estimated, actual observations on the motions of these bodies, would have proved that the theory was not accurately true.

I am willing to allow that every voluntary act is preceded by a decision of the mind, but it is strangely opposite to what I should conceive to be the just theory upon the subject, and a palpable contradiction to all experience, to say that the corporal propensities of man do not act very powerfully, as disturbing forces, in these decisions. The question, therefore, does not merely depend upon whether a man may be made to understand a distinct proposition or be convinced by an unanswerable argument. A truth may be brought home to his conviction as a rational being, though he may determine to act contrary to it, as a compound being. The cravings of hunger, the love of liquor, the desire of possessing a beautiful woman, will urge men to actions, of the fatal consequences of which, to the general interests of society, they are perfectly well convinced, even at the very time they commit them. Remove their bodily cravings, and they would not hesitate a moment in determining against such actions. Ask them their opinion of the same conduct in another person,

---

* B. 1. C. 5. P. 89.

and they would immediately reprobate it. But in their own case, and under all the circumstances of their situation with these bodily cravings, the decision of the compound being is different from the conviction of the rational being.

If this be the just view of the subject, and both theory and experience unite to prove that it is, almost all Mr. Godwin's reasonings on the subject of coercion in his 7th chapter, will appear to be founded on error. He spends some time in placing in a ridiculous point of view the attempt to convince a man's understanding and to clear up a doubtful proposition in his mind, by blows. Undoubtedly it is both ridiculous and barbarous, and so is cock-fighting, but one has little more to do with the real object of human punishments than the other. One frequent (indeed much too frequent) mode of punishment is death. Mr. Godwin will hardly think this intended for conviction, at least it does not appear how the individual or the society could reap much future benefit from an understanding enlightened in this manner.

The principal objects which human punishments have in view are undoubtedly restraint and example, restraint, or removal of an individual member whose vicious habits are likely to be prejudicial to the society. And example, which by expressing the sense of the community with regard to a particular crime, and by associating more nearly and visibly, crime and punishment, holds out a moral motive to dissuade others from the commission of it.

Restraint, Mr. Godwin thinks, may be permitted as a temporary expedient, though he reprobates solitary imprisonment, which has certainly been the most successful, and, indeed, almost the only attempt towards the moral amelioration of offenders. He talks of the selfish passions that are fostered by solitude and of the virtues generated in society. But surely these virtues are not generated in the society of a prison. Were the offender confined to the society of able and virtuous men he would probably be more improved than in solitude. But is this practicable? Mr. Godwin's ingenuity is more frequently employed in finding out evils than in suggesting practical remedies.

Punishment, for example, is totally reprobated. By endeavouring to make examples too impressive and terrible, nations have indeed, been led into the most barbarous cruelties, but the abuse of any practice is not a good argument against its use. The indefatigable pains taken in this country to find out a murder, and the certainty of its punishment, has powerfully contributed to generate that sentiment which is frequent in the mouths of the common people, that a murder will sooner or later come to light; and the habitual horror in which murder is in consequence held, will make a man, in the agony of passion, throw down his knife for fear he should be tempted to use it in the gratification of his revenge. In Italy, where murderers by flying to a sanctuary, are allowed more frequently to escape, the crime has never been held in the same detestation and has consequently been more frequent. No man, who is at all aware of the operation of moral motives, can doubt for a moment, that if every murder in Italy had been invariably punished, the use of the stilletto in transports of passion, would have been comparatively but little known.

That human laws either do, or can, proportion the punishment accurately to the offence, no person will have the folly to assert. From the inscrutability of motives the thing is absolutely impossible, but this imperfection, though it may be called a species of injustice, is no valid argument against human laws. It is the lot of man, that he will frequently have to chuse between two evils; and it is a sufficient reason for the adoption of any institution, that it is the best mode that suggests itself of preventing greater evils. A continual endeavour should undoubtedly prevail to make these institutions as perfect as the nature of them will admit. But nothing is so easy, as to find fault with human institutions; nothing so difficult, as to suggest adequate practical improvements. It is to be lamented, that more men of talents employ their time in the former occupation, than in the latter.

The frequency of crime among men, who, as the common saying is, know better, sufficiently proves, that some truths may be brought home to the conviction of the mind without always producing the proper effect upon the conduct. There are other truths of a nature that perhaps never can be adequately communicated from one man to another. The superiority of the pleasures of intellect to those of sense, Mr. Godwin considers as a fundamental truth. Taking all circumstances into consideration, I should be disposed to agree with him; but how am I to communicate this

truth to a person who has scarcely ever felt intellectual pleasure.
I may as well attempt to explain the nature and beauty of colours
to a blind man. If I am ever so laborious, patient, and clear, and
have the most repeated opportunities of expostulation, any real
progress toward the accomplishment of my purpose, seems absolutely hopeless. There is no common measure between us. I cannot
proceed step by step: it is a truth of a nature absolutely incapable
of demonstration. All that I can say is, that the wisest and best
men in all ages had agreed in giving the preference, very greatly,
to the pleasures of intellect; and that my own experience completely confirmed the truth of their decisions; that I had found
sensual pleasures vain, transient, and continually attended with
tedium and disgust; but that intellectual pleasures appeared to
me ever fresh and young, filled up all my hours satisfactorily, gave
a new zest to life, and diffused a lasting serenity over my mind.
If he believe me, it can only be from respect and veneration for
my authority: it is credulity, and not conviction. I have not said
any thing, nor can any thing be said of a nature to produce real
conviction. The affair is not an affair of reasoning, but of experience. He would probably observe in reply, what you say may be
very true with regard to yourself and many other good men, but
for my own part I feel very differently upon the subject. I have
very frequently taken up a book, and almost as frequently gone
to sleep over it; but when I pass an evening with a gay party, or a
pretty woman, I feel alive, and in spirits, and truly enjoy my
existence.

Under such circumstances, reasoning and arguments are not
instruments from which success can be expected. At some future
time perhaps, real satiety of sensual pleasures, or some accidental
impressions that awakened the energies of his mind, might effect
that, in a month, which the most patient and able expostulations,
might be incapable of effecting in forty years.

CHAPTER XIV

If the reasonings of the preceding chapter are just, the corollaries respecting political truth, which Mr. Godwin draws from the proposition, that the voluntary actions of men originate in their opinions, will not appear to be clearly established. These corollaries are, "Sound reasoning and truth, when adequately communicated, must always be victorious over error: Sound reasoning and truth are capable of being so communicated: Truth is omnipotent: The vices and moral weakness of man are not invincible. Man is perfectible, or in other words, susceptible of perpetual improvement."

The first three propositions may be considered a complete syllogism. If by adequately communicated, be meant such a conviction as to produce an adequate effect upon the conduct, the major may be allowed and the minor denied. The consequent, or the omnipotence of truth, of course falls to the ground. If by adequately communicated be meant merely the conviction of the rational faculty, the major must be denied, the minor will be only true in cases capable of demonstration, and the consequent equally falls. The fourth proposition, Mr. Godwin calls the preceding proposition, with a slight variation in the statement. If so, it must accompany the preceding proposition in its fall. But it may be worth while to inquire, with reference to the principal argument of this essay, into the particular reasons which we have for supposing that the vices and moral weakness of man can never be wholly overcome in this world.

Man, according to Mr. Godwin, is a creature, formed what he is, by the successive impressions which he has received, from the first moment that the germ from which he sprung was animated. Could he be placed in a situation, where he was subject to no evil impressions whatever, though it might be doubted whether in such a situation virtue could exist, vice would certainly be banished. The great bent of Mr. Godwin's work on political justice, if I understand it rightly, is to shew that the greater part of the vices and weaknesses of men proceed from the injustice of their political and social institutions, and that if these were removed and the understandings of men more enlightened, there would be little or no temptation in the world to evil. As it has been clearly proved, however, (at least as I think) that this is entirely a false conception, and that, independent of any political or social institutions whatever, the greater part of mankind, from the fixed and unalterable laws of nature, must ever be subject to the evil temptations arising from want, besides other passions; it follows from Mr. Godwin's definition of man that such impressions, and combinations of impressions, cannot be afloat in the world without generating a variety of bad men. According to Mr. Godwin's own conception of the formation of character, it is surely as improbable that under such circumstances, all men will be virtuous as that sixes will come up a hundred times following upon the dice. The great variety of combinations upon the dice in a repeated succession of throws, appears to me not inaptly to represent the great variety of character that must necessarily exist in the world, supposing every individual to be formed what he is, by that combination of impressions which he has received since his first existence. And this comparison will, in some measure, shew the absurdity of supposing, that exceptions will ever become general rules; that extraordinary and unusual combinations will be frequent; or that the individual instances of great virtue which have appeared in all ages of the world, will ever prevail universally.

I am aware that Mr. Godwin might say that the comparison is in one respect inaccurate, that in the case of the dice, the preceding causes, or rather the chances respecting the preceding causes, were always the same, and that, therefore, I could have no good reason for supposing that a greater number of sixes would come up in the next hundred times of throwing than in the preceding same number of throws. But, that man had in some sort a power of influencing those causes that formed character, and that every good and virtuous man that was produced, by the influence which he must necessarily have, rather increased the probability that another such virtuous character would be generated, whereas the coming up of sixes upon the dice once, would certainly not increase the probability of their coming up a second time. I admit this objection to the accuracy of the comparison, but it is only partially valid. Repeated experience has assured us, that the influence of the most virtuous character will rarely prevail against very strong temptations to evil. It will undoubtedly affect some, but it will fail with a much greater number. Had Mr. Godwin succeeded in his attempt to prove that these temptations to evil could by the exertions of man be removed, I would give up the comparison; or at least allow, that a man might be so far enlightened with regard to the mode of shaking his elbow, that he would be able to throw sixes every time. But as long as a great number of those impressions which form character, like the nice motions of the arm, remain absolutely independent of the will of man; though it would be the height of folly and presumption, to attempt to calculate the relative proportions of virtue and vice at the future periods of the world; it may be safely asserted, that the vices and moral weakness of mankind, taken in the mass, are invincible.

The fifth proposition is the general deduction from the four former and will consequently fall, as the foundations which support it have given way. In the sense in which Mr. Godwin understands the term perfectible, the perfectibility of man cannot be asserted, unless the preceding propositions could have been clearly established. There is, however, one sense, which the term will bear, in which it is, perhaps, just. It may be said with truth that man is always susceptible of improvement, or that there never has been, or will be, a period of his history, in which he can be said to have reached his possible acme of perfection. Yet it does not by any means follow from this, that our efforts to improve man will always succeed, or even, that he will ever make, in the greatest number of ages, any extraordinary strides towards perfection. The only inference that can be drawn, is that the precise limit of his improvement cannot possibly be known. And I cannot help again reminding the reader of a distinction which, it appears to me, ought particularly to be attended to in the present question: I mean, the essential difference there is, between an unlimited improvement and an improvement the limit of which cannot be ascertained. The former is an improvement not applicable to man under the present laws of his nature. The latter, undoubtedly, is applicable.

The real perfectibility of man may be illustrated, as I have mentioned before, by the perfectibility of a plant. The object of the enterprising florist is, as I conceive, to unite size, symmetry, and beauty of colour. It would surely be presumptuous in the most successful improver to affirm, that he possessed a carnation in which these qualities existed in the greatest possible state of perfection. However beautiful his flower may be, other care, other soil, or other suns, might produce one still more beautiful. Yet, although he may be aware of the absurdity of supposing that he has reached perfection; and though he may know by what means he attained that degree of beauty in the flower which he at present possesses, yet he cannot be sure that by pursuing similar means, rather increased in strength, he will obtain a more beautiful blossom. By endeavouring to improve one quality, he may impair the beauty of another. The richer mould which he would employ to increase the size of his plant, would probably burst the calyx, and destroy at once its symmetry. In a similar manner, the forcing manure used to bring about the French revolution, and to give a greater freedom and energy to the human mind, has burst the calyx of humanity, the restraining bond of all society; and, however large the separate petals have grown, however strongly, or even beautifully a few of them have been marked, the whole is at present a loose, deformed, disjointed mass, without union, symmetry, or harmony of colouring.

Were it of consequence to improve pinks and carnations, though we could have no hope of raising them as large as cabbages, we might undoubtedly expect, by successive efforts, to obtain more beautiful specimens than we at present possess. No person can deny the importance of improving the happiness of the human species. Every the least advance in this respect, is highly valuable. But an experiment with the human race is not like an experiment upon inanimate objects. The bursting of a flower may be a trifle. Another will soon succeed it. But the bursting of the bonds of society is such a separation of parts as cannot take place without giving the most acute pain to thousands: and a long time may elapse, and much misery may be endured, before the wound grows up again.

As the five propositions which I have been examining may be considered as the corner stones of Mr. Godwin's fanciful structure, and, indeed, as expressing the aim and bent of his whole work, however excellent much of his detached reasoning may be, he must be considered as having failed in the great object of his undertaking. Besides the difficulties arising from the compound nature of man, which he has by no means sufficiently smoothed, the principal argument against the perfectibility of man and society remains whole and unimpaired from any thing that he has advanced. And as far as I can trust my own judgment, this argument appears to be conclusive, not only against the perfectibility of man, in the enlarged sense in which Mr. Godwin understands the term, but against any very marked and striking change for the better, in the form and structure of general society, by which I mean, any great and decided amelioration of the condition of the lower classes of mankind, the most numerous, and, consequently, in a general view of the subject, the most important part of the human race. Were I to live a thousand years, and the laws of nature to remain the same, I should little fear, or rather little hope, a contradiction from experience in asserting that no possible sacrifices or exertions of the rich, in a country which had been long inhabited, could for any time place the lower classes of the community in a situation equal, with regard to circumstances, to the situation of the common people about thirty years ago in the northern States of America.

The lower classes of people in Europe may at some future period be much better instructed than they are at present; they may be taught to employ the little spare time they have in many better ways than at the ale-house; they may live under better and more equal laws than they have ever hitherto done, perhaps, in any country; and I even conceive it possible, though not probable, that they may have more leisure; but it is not in the nature of things, that they can be awarded such a quantity of money or subsistence, as will allow them all to marry early, in the full confidence that they shall be able to provide with ease for a numerous family.

CHAPTER XV

Mr. Godwin in the preface to his Enquirer, drops a few expressions which seem to hint at some change in his opinions since he wrote the Political Justice; and as this is a work now of some years standing, I should certainly think that I had been arguing against opinions which the author had himself seen reason to alter, but that in some of the essays of the Enquirer, Mr. Godwin's peculiar mode of thinking appears in as striking a light as ever.

It has been frequently observed that though we cannot hope to reach perfection in any thing, yet that it must always be advantageous to us to place before our eyes the most perfect models. This observation has a plausible appearance, but is very far from being generally true. I even doubt its truth in one of the most obvious exemplifications that would occur. I doubt whether a very young painter would receive so much benefit, from an attempt to copy a highly finished and perfect picture, as from copying one where the outlines were more strongly marked and the manner of laying on the colours was more easily discoverable. But in cases where the perfection of the model is a perfection of a different and superior nature from that towards which we should naturally advance, we shall not always fail in making any progress towards it, but we shall in all probability impede the progress which we might have expected to make had we not fixed our eyes upon so perfect a model. A highly intellectual being, exempt from the infirm calls of hunger or sleep, is undoubtedly a much more perfect existence than man, but were man to attempt to copy such a model, he would not only fail in making any advances towards it; but by unwisely straining to imitate what was inimitable, he would probably destroy the little intellect which he was endeavouring to improve.

The form and structure of society which Mr. Godwin describes is as essentially distinct from any forms of society which have hitherto prevailed in the world, as a being that can live without food or sleep is from a man. By improving society in its present form, we are making no more advances towards such a state of things as he pictures, than we should make approaches towards a line, with regard to which we were walking parallel. The question, therefore is, whether, by looking to such a form of society as our polar star, we are likely to advance or retard the improvement of the human species? Mr. Godwin appears to me to have decided this question against himself in his essay on avarice and profusion in the Enquirer.

Dr. Adam Smith has very justly observed that nations as well as individuals grow rich by parsimony and poor by profusion, and that, therefore, every frugal man was a friend and every spendthrift an enemy to his country. The reason he gives is that what is saved from revenue is always added to stock, and is therefore taken from the maintenance of labour that is generally unproductive and employed in the maintenance of labour that realizes itself in valuable commodities. No observation can be more evidently just. The subject of Mr. Godwin's essay is a little similar in its first appearance, but in essence is as distinct as possible. He considers the mischief of profusion as an acknowledged truth, and therefore makes his comparison between the avaricious man, and the man who spends his income. But the avaricious man of Mr. Godwin is totally a distinct character, at least with regard to his effect upon the prosperity of the state, from the frugal man of Dr. Adam Smith. The frugal man in order to make more money saves from his income and adds to his capital, and this capital he either employs himself in the maintenance of productive labour, or he lends it to some other person who will probably employ it in this way. He benefits the state because he adds to its general capital, and because wealth employed as capital, not only sets in motion more labour, than when spent as income, but the labour is besides of a more valuable kind. But the avaricious man of Mr. Godwin locks up his wealth in a chest and sets in motion no labour of any kind, either productive or unproductive. This is so essential a difference that Mr. Godwin's decision in his essay appears at once as evidently false as Dr. Adam Smith's position is evidently true. It could not, indeed, but occur to Mr. Godwin, that some present inconvenience might arise to the poor, from thus locking up the funds destined for the maintenance of labour. The only way, therefore, he had of weakening this objection was to compare the two characters chiefly with regard to their tendency to accelerate the approach of that happy state of cultivated equality, on which he says we ought always to fix our eyes as our polar star.

I think it has been proved in the former parts of this essay that such a state of society is absolutely impracticable. What consequences then are we to expect from looking to such a point as our guide and polar star in the great sea of political discovery? Reason would teach us to expect no other, than winds perpetually adverse, constant but fruitless toil, frequent shipwreck, and certain misery. We shall not only fail in making the smallest real approach towards such a perfect form of society; but by wasting our strength of mind and body, in a direction in which it is impossible to proceed, and by the frequent distress which we must necessarily occasion by our repeated failures, we shall evidently impede that degree of improvement in society, which is really attainable.

It has appeared that a society constituted according to Mr. Godwin's system must, from the inevitable laws of our nature, degenerate into a class of proprietors and a class of labourers, and that the substitution of benevolence for self-love as the moving principle of society, instead of producing the happy effects that might be expected from so fair a name, would cause the same pressure of want to be felt by the whole of society, which is now felt only by a part. It is to the established administration of property and to the apparently narrow principle of self-love that we are indebted for all the noblest exertions of human genius, all the finer and more delicate emotions of the soul, for everything, indeed, that distinguishes the civilized, from the savage state; and no sufficient change, has as yet taken place in the nature of civilized man, to enable us to say, that he either is, or ever will be, in a state, when he may safely throw down the ladder by which he has risen to this eminence.

If in every society that has advanced beyond the savage state, a class of proprietors and a class of labourers* must necessarily exist, it is evident that, as labour is the only property of the class of labourers, every thing that tends to diminish the value of this property, must tend to diminish the possessions of this part of society. The only way that a poor man has of supporting himself in independence, is by the exertion of his bodily strength. This is the only commodity he has to give in exchange for the necessaries of life. It would harldy appear then that you benefit him, by narrowing the market for this commodity, by decreasing the demand for labour, and lessening the value of the only property that he possesses.

Mr. Godwin would perhaps say that the whole system of barter and exchange is a vile and iniquitous traffic. If you would essentially relieve the poor man, you should take a part of his labour upon yourself, or give him your money, without exacting so severe a return for it. In answer to the first method proposed, it may be observed, that even if the rich could be persuaded to assist the poor in this way, the value of the assistance would be comparatively trifling. The rich, though they think themselves of great importance bear but a small proportion in point of numbers to the poor, and would, therefore, relieve them but of a small part of their burdens by taking a share. Were all those that are employed in the labours of luxuries, added to the number of those employed in producing necessaries; and could these necessary labours be amicably divided among all, each man's share might indeed be comparatively light; but desirable as such an amicable division would undoubtedly be, I cannot conceive any practical principle†

---

* It should be observed that the principal argument of this essay only goes to prove the necessity of a class of proprietors, and a class of labourers, but by no means infers that the present great inequality of property is either necessary or useful to society. On the contrary, it must certainly be considered as an evil, and every institution that promotes it is essentially bad and impolitic. But whether a government could with advantage to society actively interfere to repress inequality of fortunes, may be a matter of doubt. Perhaps the generous system of perfect liberty, adopted by Dr. Adam Smith, and the French economists, would be ill exchanged for any system of restraint.

† Mr. Godwin seems to have but little respect for practical principles; but I own it appears to me, that he is a much greater benefactor to mankind, who points out how an inferior good may be attained, than he who merely expatiates on the deformity of the present state of society, and the beauty of a different state, without pointing out a practical method, that might be immediately applied, of accelerating our advances from the one, to the other.

according to which it could take place. It has been shewn, that the spirit of benevolence, guided by the strict impartial justice that Mr. Godwin describes, would, if vigorously acted upon, depress in want and misery the whole human race. Let us examine what would be the consequence, if the proprietor were to retain a decent share for himself; but to give the rest away to the poor, without exacting a task from them in return. Not to mention the idleness and the vice that such a proceeding, if general, would probably create in the present state of society, and the great risk there would be, of diminishing the produce of land, as well as the labours of luxury, another objection yet remains.

It has appeared that from the principle of population more will always be in want than can be adequately supplied. The surplus of the rich man might be sufficient for three, but four will be desirous to obtain it. He cannot make this selection of three out of the four without conferring a great favour on those that are the objects of his choice. These persons must consider themselves as under a great obligation to him and as dependent upon his for their support. The rich man would feel his power and the poor man his dependence, and the evil effects of these two impressions on the human heart are well known. Though I perfectly agree with Mr. Godwin therefore in the evil of hard labour, yet I still think it a less evil, and less calculated to debase the human mind, than dependence, and every history of man that we have ever read, places in a strong point of view the danger to which that mind is exposed, which is intrusted with constant power.

In the present state of things, and particularly when labour is in request, the man who does a days work for me confers full as great an obligation upon me as I do upon him. I possess what he wants, he possesses what I want. We make an amicable exchange. The poor man walks erect in conscious independence; and the mind of his employer is not vitiated by a sense of power.

Three or four hundred years ago, there was undoubtedly much less labour in England, in proportion to the population than at present, but there was much more dependence, and we probably should not now enjoy our present degree of civil liberty if the poor, by the introduction of manufactures, had not been enabled to give something in exchange for the provisions of the great Lords, instead of being dependent upon their bounty. Even the greatest enemies of trade and manufactures, and I do not reckon myself a very determined friend to them, must allow that when they were introduced into England, liberty came in their train.

Nothing that has been said tends in the most remote degree to undervalue the principle of benevolence. It is one of the noblest and most godlike qualities of the human heart, generated perhaps, slowly and gradually from self-love, and afterwards intended to act as a general law, whose kind office it should be, to soften the partial deformities, to correct the asperities, and to smooth the wrinkles of its parent: and this seems to be the analogy of all nature. Perhaps there is no one general law of nature that will not appear, to us at least, to produce partial evil; and we frequently observe at the same time, some bountiful provision, which acting as another general law, corrects the inequalities of the first.

The proper office of benevolence is to soften the partial evils arising from self-love, but it can never be substituted in its place. If no man were to allow himself to act till he had completely determined that the action he was about to perform was more conducive than any other to the general good, the most enlightened minds would hesitate in perplexity and amazement; and the unenlightened would be continually committing the grossest mistakes.

As Mr. Godwin, therefore, has not laid down any practical principle according to which the necessary labours of agriculture might be amicably shared among the whole class of labourers, by general invectives against employing the poor he appears to pursue an unattainable good through much present evil. For if every man who employs the poor ought to be considered as their enemy, and as adding to the weight of their oppressions, and if the miser is for this reason to be preferred to the man who spends his income, it follows that any number of men who now spend their incomes might, to the advantage of society, be converted into misers. Suppose then that a hundred thousand persons who now employ ten men each were to lock up their wealth from general use, it is evident, that a million of working men of different kinds would be completely thrown out of all employment. The extensive misery that such an event would produce in the present state of society,

Mr. Godwin himself could hardly refuse to acknowledge, and I question whether he might not find some difficulty in proving that a conduct of this kind tended more than the conduct of those who spend their incomes to "place human beings in the condition in which they ought to be placed."

But Mr. Godwin says that the miser really locks up nothing, that the point has not been rightly understood, and that the true development and definition of the nature of wealth have not been applied to illustrate it. Having defined therefore wealth, very justly, to be the commodities raised and fostered by human labour, he observes that the miser locks up neither corn, nor oxen, nor clothes, nor houses. Undoubtedly he does not really lock up these articles, but he locks up the power of producing them, which is virtually the same. These things are certainly used and consumed by his contemporaries, as truly, and to as great an extent, as if he were a beggar; but not to as great an extent, as if he had employed his wealth in turning up more land, in breeding more oxen, in employing more taylors, and in building more houses. But supposing, for a moment, that the conduct of the miser did not tend to check any really useful produce, how are all those, who are thrown out of employment, to obtain patents which they may shew in order to be awarded a proper share of the food and raiment produced by the society? This is the unconquerable difficulty.

I am perfectly willing to concede to Mr. Godwin that there is much more labour in the world than is really necessary, and that, if the lower classes of society could agree among themselves never to work more than six or seven hours in the day, the commodities essential to human happiness might still be produced in as great abundance as at present. But it is almost impossible to conceive that such an agreement could be adhered to. From the principle of population, some would necessarily be more in want than others. Those that had large families would naturally be desirous of exchanging two hours more of their labour for an ampler quantity of subsistence. How are they to be prevented from making this exchange? It would be a violation of the first and most sacred property that a man possesses, to attempt, by positive institutions, to interfere with his command over his own labour.

Till Mr. Godwin, therefore, can point out some practical plan

according to which the necessary labour in a society might be
equitably divided, his invectives against labour, if they were at
tended to, would certainly produce much present evil without
approximating us to that state of cultivated equality to which he
looks forward as his polar star, and which, he seems to think,
should at present be our guide in determining the nature and
tendency of human actions. A mariner guided by such a polar star
is in danger of shipwreck.

Perhaps there is no possible way in which wealth could in general be employed so beneficially to a state, and particularly to the
lower orders of it, as by improving and rendering productive that
land which to a farmer would not answer the expence of cultivation. Had Mr. Godwin exerted his energetic eloquence in painting
the superior worth and usefulness of the character who employed
the poor in this way, to him who employed them in narrow luxuries, every enlightened man must have applauded his efforts. The
increasing demand for agricultural labour must always tend to
better the condition of the poor; and if the accession of work be
of this kind, so far is it from being true, that the poor would be
obliged to work ten hours for the same price that they before
worked eight, that the very reverse would be the fact; and a
labourer might then support his wife and family as well by the
labour of six hours, as he could before by the labour of eight.

The labour created by luxuries, though useful in distributing
the produce of the country, without vitiating the proprietor by
power, or debasing the labourer by dependence, has not, indeed,
the same beneficial effects on the state of the poor. A great accession of work from manufacturers, though it may raise the price of
labour even more than an increasing demand for agricultural
labour; yet, as in this case, the quantity of food in the country may
not be proportionably increasing, the advantage to the poor will
be but temporary, as the price of provisions must necessarily rise
in proportion to the price of labour. Relative to this subject, I
cannot avoid venturing a few remarks on a part of Dr. Adam
Smith's Wealth of Nations, speaking at the same time with that
diffidence which I ought certainly to feel in differing from a person
so justly celebrated in the political world.

CHAPTER XVI

The professed object of Dr. Adam Smith's inquiry is the nature and causes of the wealth of nations. There is another inquiry, however, perhaps still more interesting, which he occasionally mixes with it, I mean an inquiry into the causes which affect the happiness of nations or the happiness and comfort of the lower orders of society, which is the most numerous class in every nation. I am sufficiently aware of the near connection of these two subjects, and that the causes which tend to increase the wealth of a State, tend also, generally speaking, to increase the happiness of the lower classes of the people. But perhaps Dr. Adam Smith has considered these two inquiries as still more nearly connected than they really are; at least, he has not stopped to take notice of those instances where the wealth of a society may increase (according to his definition of wealth) without having any tendency to increase the comforts of the labouring part of it. I do not mean to enter into a philosophical discussion of what constitutes the proper happiness of man, but shall merely consider two universally acknowledged ingredients, health, and the command of the necessaries and conveniences of life.

Little or no doubt can exist that the comforts of the labouring poor depend upon the increase of the funds destined for the maintenance of labour, and will be very exactly in proportion to the rapidity of this increase. The demand for labour which such increase would occasion, by creating a competition in the market, must necessarily raise the value of labour, and, till the additional number of hands required were reared, the increased funds would be distributed to the same number of persons as before the increase, and therefore every labourer would live comparatively at his ease. But perhaps Dr. Adam Smith errs in representing every increase of the revenue or stock of a society as an increase of these funds. Such surplus stock or revenue will, indeed, always be considered by the individual possessing it, as an additional fund from which he may maintain more labour: but it will not be a real and effectual fund for the maintenance of an additional number of labourers, unless the whole, or at least a great part of this increase of the stock or revenue of the society, be convertible into a proportional quantity of provisions; and it will not be so convertible, where the increase has arisen merely from the produce of labour, and not from the produce of land. A distinction will in this case occur, between the number of hands which the stock of the society could employ, and the number which its territory can maintain.

To explain myself by an instance. Dr. Adam Smith defines the wealth of a nation to consist in the annual produce of its land and labour. This definition evidently includes manufactured produce, as well as the produce of the land. Now supposing a nation for a course of years was to add what it saved from its yearly revenue to its manufacturing capital solely, and not to its capital employed upon land, it is evident that it might grow richer according to the above definition, without a power of supporting a greater number of labourers, and therefore, without an increase in the real funds for the maintenance of labour. There would, notwithstanding, be a demand for labour from the power which each manufacturer would possess, or at least think he possessed, of extending his old stock in trade or of setting up fresh works. This demand would of course raise the price of labour, but if the yearly stock of provisions in the country was not increasing, this rise would soon turn out to be merely nominal, as the price of provisions must necessarily rise with it. The demand for manufacturing labourers might, indeed, entice many from agriculture and thus tend to diminish the annual produce of the land, but we will suppose any effect of this kind to be compensated by improvements in the instruments of agriculture, and the quantity of provisions therefore to remain the same. Improvements in manufacturing machinery would of course take place, and this circumstance, added to the greater number of hands employed in manufactures, would cause the annual produce of the labour of the country to be upon the whole greatly increased. The wealth therefore of the country would be increasing annually, according to the definition, and might not, perhaps, be increasing very slowly.

The question is whether wealth, increasing in this way, has any tendency to better the condition of the labouring poor. It is a self-evident proposition that any general rise in the price of labour, the stock of provisions remaining the same, can only be a nominal rise, as it must very shortly be followed by a proportional rise in provisions. The increase in the price of labour therefore, which we have supposed, would have little or no effect in giving the labouring poor a greater command over the necessaries and conveniences of life. In this respect they would be nearly in the same state as before. In one other respect they would be in a worse state. A greater proportion of them would be employed in manufactures, and fewer, consequently, in agriculture. And this exchange of professions will be allowed, I think, by all, to be very unfavourable in respect of health, one essential ingredient of happiness, besides the greater uncertainty of manufacturing labour, arising from the capricious taste of man, the accidents of war, and other causes.

It may be said, perhaps, that such an instance as I have supposed could not occur, because the rise in the price of provisions would immediately turn some additional capital into the channel of agriculture. But this is an event which may take place very slowly, as it should be remarked, that a rise in the price of labour, had preceded the rise of provisions, and would, therefore, impede the good effects upon agriculture, which the increased value of the produce of the land might otherwise have occasioned.

It might also be said, that the additional capital of the nation would enable it to import provisions sufficient for the maintenance of those whom its stock could employ. A small country with a large navy, and great inland accommodations for carriage, such as Holland, may, indeed, import and distribute an effectual quantity of provisions; but the price of provisions must be very high to make such an importation and distribution answer in large countries less advantageously circumstanced in this respect.

An instance, accurately such as I have supposed, may not, perhaps, ever have occurred, but I have little doubt that instances nearly approximating to it may be found without any very laborious search. Indeed I am strongly inclined to think that England herself, since the revolution affords a very striking elucidation of the argument in question.

The commerce of this country, internal as well as external, has certainly been rapidly advancing during the last century. The exchangeable value in the market of Europe of the annual produce of its land and labour has, without doubt, increased very considerably. But, upon examination, it will be found that the increase has been chiefly in the produce of labour and not in the produce of land, and therefore, though the wealth of the nation has been advancing with a quick pace, the effectual funds for the maintenance of labour have been increasing very slowly, and the result is such as might be expected. The increasing wealth of the nation has had little or no tendency to better the condition of the labouring poor. They have not, I believe, a greater command of the necessaries and conveniences of life, and a much greater proportion of them than at the period of the revolution is employed in manufactures and crowded together in close and unwholesome rooms.

Could we believe the statement of Dr. Price that the population of England has decreased since the revolution, it would even appear that the effectual funds for the maintenance of labour had been declining during the progress of wealth in other respects. For I conceive that it may be laid down as a general rule that if the effectual funds for the maintenance of labour are increasing, that is, if the territory can maintain as well as the stock employ a greater number of labourers, this additional number will quickly spring up, even in spite of such wars as Dr. Price enumerates. And, consequently, if the population of any country has been stationary, or declining, we may safely infer, that, however it may have advanced in manufacturing wealth, its effectual funds for the maintenance of labour cannot have increased.

It is difficult, however, to conceive that the population of England has been declining since the revolution, though every testimony concurs to prove that its increase, if it has increased, has been very slow. In the controversy which the question has occasioned, Dr. Price undoubtedly appears to be much more completely master of his subject, and to possess more accurate information than his opponents. Judging simply from this controversy, I think one should say that Dr. Price's point is nearer being proved than Mr. Howlett's. Truth, probably, lies between the two statements, but this supposition makes the increase of population since the revolution to have been very slow in comparison with the increase of wealth.

That the produce of the land has been decreasing, or even that it has been absolutely stationary during the last century, few will be disposed to believe. The inclosure of commons and waste lands certainly tends to increase the food of the country, but it has been asserted with confidence that the inclosure of common fields has frequently had a contrary effect, and that large tracts of land which formerly produced great quantities of corn, by being converted into pasture, both employ fewer hands and feed fewer mouths than before their inclosure. It is, indeed, an acknowledged truth, that pasture land produces a smaller quantity of human subsistence than corn land of the same natural fertility, and could it be clearly ascertained that from the increased demand for butchers meat of the best quality, and its increased price in consequence, a greater quantity of good land has annually been employed in grazing, the diminution of human subsistence, which this circumstance would occasion, might have counterbalanced the advantages derived from the inclosure of waste lands, and the general improvements in husbandry.

It scarcely need be remarked that the high price of butchers meat at present, and its low price formerly, were not caused by the scarcity in the one case or the plenty in the other, but by the different expence sustained at the different periods, in preparing cattle for the market. It is, however, possible, that there might have been more cattle a hundred years ago in the country, than at present; but no doubt can be entertained, that there is much more meat of a superior quality brought to market at present, than ever there was. When the price of butchers meat was very low, cattle were reared chiefly upon waste lands; and except for some of the principal markets, were probably killed with but little other fatting. The veal that is sold so cheap in some distant counties at present, bears little other resemblance than the name, to that which is bought in London. Formerly, the price of butchers meat would not pay for rearing, and scarcely for feeding cattle on land that would answer in tillage; but the present price will not only pay for fatting cattle on the very best land, but will even allow of the rearing many, on land that would bear good crops of corn.

The same number of cattle, or even the same weight of cattle at the different periods when killed, will have consumed (if I may be allowed the expression) very different quantities of human subsistence. A fatted beast may in some respects be considered, in the language of the French economists, as an unproductive labourer: he has added nothing to the value of the raw produce that he has consumed. The present system of grazing, undoubtedly tends more than the former system to diminish the quantity of human subsistence in the country, in proportion to the general fertility of the land.

I would not by any means be understood to say that the former system either could or ought to have continued. The increasing price of butchers meat is a natural and inevitable consequence of the general progress of cultivation; but I cannot help thinking, that the present great demand for butchers meat of the best quality, and the quantity of good land that is in consequence annually employed to produce it, together with the great number of horses at present kept for pleasure, are the chief causes, that have prevented the quantity of human food in the country, from keeping pace with the generally increased fertility of the soil; and a change of custom in these respects, would, I have little doubt, have a very sensible effect on the quantity of subsistence in the country, and consequently on its population.

The employment of much of the most fertile land in grazing, the improvements in agricultural instruments, the increase of large farms, and particularly the diminution of the number of cottages throughout the kingdom, all concur to prove, that there are not probably so many persons employed in agricultural labour now as at the period of the revolution. Whatever increase of population, therefore, has taken place, must be employed almost wholly in manufactures, and it is well known that the failure of some of these manufactures, merely from the caprice of fashion, such as the adoption of muslins instead of silks, or of shoe-strings and covered buttons, instead of buckles and metal buttons, combined with the restraints in the market of labour arising from corporation, and parish laws, have frequently driven thousands on charity for support. The great increase of the poor rates is, indeed, of itself a strong evidence that the poor have not a greater

command of the necessaries and conveniences of life, and if to the
consideration, that their condition in this respect is rather worse
than better, be added the circumstance, that a much greater proportion of them is employed in large manufactories, unfavourable
both to health and virtue, it must be acknowledged, that the
increase of wealth of late years, has had no tendency to increase
the happiness of the labouring poor.

That every increase of the stock or revenue of a nation cannot
be considered as an increase of the real funds for the maintenance
of labour and, therefore, cannot have the same good effect upon
the condition of the poor will appear in a strong light if the
argument be applied to China.

Dr. Adam Smith observes that China has probably long been
as rich as the nature of her laws and institutions will admit, but
that with other laws and institutions, and if foreign commerce
were had in honour, she might still be much richer. The question
is, would such an increase of wealth be an increase of the real funds
for the maintenance of labour, and consequently, tend to place the
lower classes of people in China in a state of greater plenty?

It is evident, that if trade and foreign commerce were held in
great honour in China, from the plenty of labourers, and the
cheapness of labour she might work up manufactures for foreign
sale to an immense amount. It is equally evident that from the
great bulk of provisions and the amazing extent of her inland
territory she could not in return import such a quantity as would
be any sensible addition to the annual stock of subsistence in the
country. Her immense amount of manufactures, therefore, she
would exchange, chiefly, for luxuries collected from all parts of
the world. At present, it appears, that no labour whatever is
spared in the production of food. The country is rather over
peopled in proportion to what its stock can employ, and labour is,
therefore, so abundant, that no pains are taken to abridge it. The
consequence of this is, probably, the greatest production of food
that the soil can possibly afford, for it will be generally observed,
that processes for abridging labour, though they may enable a
farmer to bring a certain quantity of grain cheaper to market, tend
rather to diminish, than increase the whole produce; and in agriculture, therefore, may, in some respects, be considered rather as
private, than public advantages.

An immense capital could not be employed in China in preparing manufactures for foreign trade without taking off so many labourers from agriculture as to alter this state of things, and in some degree to diminish the produce of the country. The demand for manufacturing labourers would naturally raise the price of labour, but as the quantity of subsistence would not be increased, the price of provisions would keep pace with it, or even more than keep pace with it if the quantity of provisions were really decreasing. The country would be evidently advancing in wealth, the exchangeable value of the annual produce of its land and labour would be annually augmented, yet the real funds for the maintenance of labour would be stationary, or even declining, and, consequently, the increasing wealth of the nation would rather tend to depress than to raise the condition of the poor. With regard to the command over the necessaries and comforts of life, they would be in the same or rather worse state than before; and a great part of them would have exchanged the healthy labours of agriculture, for the unhealthy occupations of manufacturing industry.

The argument, perhaps, appears clearer when applied to China, because it is generally allowed that the wealth of China has been long stationary. With regard to any other country it might be always a matter of dispute at which of the two periods, compared, wealth was increasing the fastest, as it is upon the rapidity of the increase of wealth at any particular period, that Dr. Adam Smith says the condition of the poor depends. It is evident, however, that two nations might increase exactly with the same rapidity in the exchangeable value of the annual produce of their land and labour, yet if one had applied itself chiefly to agriculture, and the other chiefly to commerce, the funds for the maintenance of labour, and consequently the effect of the increase of wealth in each nation, would be extremely different. In that which had applied itself chiefly to agriculture, the poor would live in great plenty, and population would rapidly increase. In that which had applied itself chiefly to commerce, the poor would be comparatively but little benefited and consequently population would increase slowly.

CHAPTER XVII

A question seems naturally to arise here whether the exchangeable value of the annual produce of the land and labour be the proper definition of the wealth of a country, or whether the gross produce of the land, according to the French economists, may not be a more accurate definition. Certain it is that every increase of wealth, according to the definition of the economists, will be an increase of the funds for the maintenance of labour, and consequently will always tend to ameliorate the condition of the labouring poor, though an increase of wealth, according to Dr. Adam Smith's definition, will by no means invariably have the same tendency. And yet it may not follow from this consideration that Dr. Adam Smith's definition is not just. It seems in many respects improper to exclude the clothing and lodging of a whole people from any part of their revenue. Much of it may, indeed, be of very trivial and unimportant value in comparison with the food of the country, yet still it may be fairly considered as a part of its revenue, and, therefore, the only point in which I should differ from Dr. Adam Smith, is where he seems to consider every increase of the revenue or stock of a society as an increase of the funds for the maintenance of labour, and consequently, as tending always to ameliorate the condition of the poor.

The fine silks and cottons, the laces, and other ornamental luxuries of a rich country may contribute very considerably to augment the exchangeable value of its annual produce; yet they contribute but in a very small degree to augment the mass of happiness in the society, and it appears to me that it is with some view to the real utility of the produce that we ought to estimate the productiveness, or unproductiveness of different sorts of labour.

The French economists consider all labour employed in manufactures as unproductive. Comparing it with the labour employed upon land, I should be perfectly disposed to agree with them, but not exactly for the reasons which they give. They say that labour employed upon land is productive because the produce, over and above completely paying the labourer and the farmer, affords a clear rent to the landlord, and that the labour employed upon a piece of lace is unproductive because it merely replaces the provisions that the workman had consumed, and the stock of his employer, without affording any clear rent whatever. But supposing the value of the wrought lace to be such, as that besides paying in the most complete manner the workman and his employer, it could afford a clear rent to a third person; it appears to me, that in comparison with the labour employed upon land, it would be still as unproductive as ever. Though according to the reasoning used by the French economists, the man employed in the manufacture of lace would, in this case, seem to be a productive labourer; yet according to their definition of the wealth of a state, he ought not to be considered in that light. He will have added nothing to the gross produce of the land: he has consumed a portion of this gross produce, and has left a bit of lace in return; and though he may sell this bit of lace for three times the quantity of provisions that he consumed whilst he was making it, and thus be a very productive labourer with regard to himself; yet he cannot be considered as having added by his labour to any essential part of the riches of the state. The clear rent, therefore, that a certain produce can afford, after paying the expences of procuring it, does not appear to be the sole criterion, by which to judge of the productiveness or unproductiveness to a state of any particular species of labour.

Suppose that two hundred thousand men, who are now employed in producing manufactures that only tend to gratify the vanity of a few rich people, were to be employed upon some barren and uncultivated lands, and to produce only half the quantity of food that they themselves consumed; they would be still, more productive labourers with regard to the state than they were before, though their labour, so far from affording a rent to a third person, would but half replace the provisions used in obtaining the produce. In their former employment they consumed a certain portion of the food of the country and left in return some silks and laces. In their latter employment they consumed the same quantity of food and left in return provision for a hundred thousand men. There can be little doubt which of the two legacies would be the most really beneficial to the country, and it will, I think, be allowed that the wealth which supported the two hundred thousand men while they were producing silks and laces would have been more usefully employed in supporting them while they were producing the additional quantity of food.

A capital employed upon land may be unproductive to the individual that employs it and yet be highly productive to the society. A capital employed in trade on the contrary, may be highly productive to the individual, and yet be almost totally unproductive to the society: and this is the reason why I should call manufacturing labour unproductive, in comparison of that which is employed in agriculture, and not for the reason given by the French economists. It is, indeed, almost impossible, to see the great fortunes that are made in trade, and the liberality with which so many merchants live, and yet agree in the statement of the economists, that manufacturers can only grow rich by depriving themselves of the funds destined for their support. In many branches of trade the profits are so great, as would allow of a clear rent to a third person; but as there is no third person in the case, and as all the profits centre in the master manufacturer, or merchant, he seems to have a fair chance of growing rich, without much privation; and we consequently see large fortunes acquired in trade by persons who have not been remarked for their parsimony.

Daily experience proves that the labour employed in trade and manufactures is sufficiently productive to individuals, but it certainly is not productive in the same degree to the state. Every accession to the food of a country, tends to the immediate benefit of the whole society; but the fortunes made in trade, tend, but in a remote and uncertain manner, to the same end, and in some respects have even a contrary tendency. The home trade of consumption, is by far the most important trade of every nation. China is the richest country in the world, without any other. Putting then, for a moment, foreign trade out of the question, the man, who by an engenious manufacture, obtains a double portion out of the old stock of provisions, will certainly not be so useful to the state, as the man who, by his labour, adds a single share to the former stock. The consumable commodities of silks, laces, trinkets, and expensive furniture, are undoubtedly a part of the revenue of the society; but they are the revenue only of the rich, and not of the society in general. An increase in this part of the revenue of a state, cannot, therefore be considered of the same importance, as an increase of food, which forms the principal revenue of the great mass of the people.

Foreign commerce adds to the wealth of a state, according to Dr. Adam Smith's definition, though not according to the definition of the economists. Its principal use, and the reason, probably that it has in general been held in such high estimation is that it adds greatly to the external power of a nation or to its power of commanding the labour of other countries; but it will be found, upon a near examination, to contribute but little to the increase of the internal funds for the maintenance of labour, and consequently but little to the happiness of the greatest part of society. In the natural progress of a state towards riches, manufactures, and foreign commerce; would follow, in their order, the high cultivation of the soil. In Europe, this natural order of things has been inverted, and the soil has been cultivated from the redundancy of manufacturing capital, instead of manufactures rising from the redundancy of capital employed upon land. The superior encouragement that has been given to the industry of the towns, and the consequent higher price that is paid for the labour of artificers, than for the labour of those employed in husbandry, are probably the reasons why so much soil in Europe remains uncultivated. Had a different policy been pursued throughout Europe, it might undoubtedly have been much more populous than at present, and yet not be more incumbered by its population.

I cannot quit this curious subject of the difficulty arising from population, a subject that appears to me to deserve a minute investigation and able discussion much beyond my power to give it, without taking notice of an extraordinary passage in Dr. Price's two volumes of Observations. Having given some tables on the probabilities of life, in towns and in the country, he says,* "From this comparison, it appears, with how much truth great cities have been called the graves of mankind. It must also convince all who consider it, that according to the observation, at the end of the fourth essay, in the former volume, it is by no means strictly proper to consider our diseases as the original intention of nature. They are, without doubt, in general our own creation. *Were there a country where the inhabitants led lives entirely natural and virtuous, few of them would die without measuring out the whole period of present existence allotted to them; pain and distemper would be unknown among them, and death would come upon them like a sleep, in consequence of no other cause than gradual and unavoidable decay."*

I own that I felt myself obliged to draw a very opposite conclusion from the facts advanced in Dr. Price's two volumes. I had for some time been aware that population and food increased in different ratios, and a vague opinion had been floating in my mind that they could only be kept equal by some species of misery or vice, but the perusal of Dr. Price's two volumes of Observations, after that opinion had been conceived, raised it at once to conviction. With so many facts in his view to prove the extraordinary rapidity with which population increases when unchecked, and with such a body of evidence before him to elucidate, even the manner by which the general laws of nature repress a redundant population, it is perfectly inconceivable to me how he could write the passage that I have quoted. He was a strenuous advocate for early marriages, as the best preservative against vicious manners. He had no fanciful conceptions about the extinction of the passion between the sexes, like Mr. Godwin, nor did he ever think of eluding the difficulty in the ways hinted at by Mr. Condorcet. He frequently talks of giving the prolifick powers of nature room to exert themselves. Yet with these ideas, that his understanding could escape from the obvious and necessary inference that an unchecked population would increase, beyond comparison, faster than the earth, by the best directed exertions of man, could produce food for its support, appears to me as astonishing, as if he

---

* Vol. 2, page 243.

had resisted the conclusion of one of the plainest propositions of Euclid.

Dr. Price, speaking of the different stages of the civilized state, says, "The first, or simple stages of civilization, are those which favour most the increase and the happiness of mankind." He then instances the American colonies, as being at that time in the first and happiest of the states that he had described, and as affording a very striking proof of the effects of the different stages of civilization on population. But he does not seem to be aware that the happiness of the Americans depended much less upon their peculiar degree of civilization than upon the peculiarity of their situation, as new colonies, upon their having a great plenty of fertile uncultivated land. In parts of Norway, Denmark, or Sweden, or in this country, two or three hundred years ago, he might have found perhaps nearly the same degree of civilization, but by no means the same happiness or the same increase of population. He quotes himself a statute of Henry the Eighth, complaining of the decay of tillage, and the enhanced price of provisions, "whereby a marvellous number of people were rendered incapable of maintaining themselves and families." The superior degree of civil liberty which prevailed in America, contributed, without doubt, its share to promote the industry, happiness, and population of these states, but even civil liberty, all powerful as it is, will not create fresh land. The Americans may be said, perhaps, to enjoy a greater degree of civil liberty, now they are an independent people, than while they were in subjection to England, but we may be perfectly sure that population will not long continue to increase with the same rapidity as it did then.

A person who contemplated the happy state of the lower classes of people in America twenty years ago would naturally wish to retain them for ever in that state, and might think, perhaps, that by preventing the introduction of manufactures and luxury he might effect his purpose, but he might as reasonably expect to prevent a wife or mistress from growing old by never exposing her to the sun or air. The situation of new colonies, well governed, is a bloom of youth that no efforts can arrest. There are, indeed, many modes of treatment in the political, as well as animal body, that contribute to accelerate or retard the approaches of age, but there can be no chance of success, in any mode that could be divised, for keeping either of them in perpetual youth. By encouraging the industry of the towns more than the industry of the country, Europe may be said, perhaps, to have brought on a premature old age. A different policy in this respect, would infuse fresh life and vigour into every state. While from the law of primogeniture, and other European customs, land bears a monopoly price, a capital can never be employed in it with much advantage to the individual; and, therefore, it is not probable that the soil should be properly cultivated. And, though in every civilized state, a class of proprietors and a class of labourers must exist; yet one permanent advantage would always result from a nearer equalization of property. The greater the number of proprietors, the smaller must be the number of labourers: a greater part of society would be in the happy state of possessing property; and a smaller part in the unhappy state of possessing no other property than their labour. But the best directed exertions, though they may alleviate, can never remove the pressure of want, and it will be difficult for any person who contemplates the genuine situation of man on earth, and the general laws of nature, to suppose it possible that any, the most enlightened efforts, could place mankind in a state where "few would die without measuring out the whole period of present existence allotted to them; where pain and distemper would be unknown among them; and death would come upon them like a sleep, in consequence of no other cause than gradual and unavoidable decay."

It is, undoubtedly a most disheartening reflection that the great obstacle in the way to any extraordinary improvement in society is of a nature that we can never hope to overcome. The perpetual tendency in the race of man to increase beyond the means of subsistence is one of the general laws of animated nature which we can have no reason to expect will change. Yet, discouraging as the contemplation of this difficulty must be to those whose exertions are laudably directed to the improvement of the human species, it is evident that no possible good can arise from any endeavours to slur it over or keep it in the back ground. On the contrary, the most baleful mischiefs may be expected from the unmanly conduct of not daring to face truth because it is unpleasing. Independently of what relates to this great obstacle, sufficient yet remains to be done for mankind to animate us to the most unremitted exertion. But if we proceed without a thorough knowledge and accurate comprehension of the nature, extent, and magnitude of the difficulties we have to encounter, or if we unwisely direct our efforts towards an object, in which we cannot hope for success, we shall not only exhaust our strength in fruitless exertions and remain at as great a distance as ever from the summit of our wishes, but we shall be perpetually crushed by the recoil of this rock of Sisyphus.

CHAPTER XVIII

The view of human life which results from the contemplation of the constant pressure of distress on man from the difficulty of subsistence, by shewing the little expectation that he can reasonably entertain of perfectibility on earth, seems strongly to point his hopes to the future. And the temptations to which he must necessarily be exposed from the operation of those laws of nature which we have been examining,, would seem to represent the world in the light in which it has been frequently considered, as a state of trial and school of virtue preparatory to a superior state of happiness. But I hope I shall be pardoned if I attempt to give a view in some degree different of the situation of man on earth, which appears to me to be more consistent with the various phenomena of nature which we observe around us and more consonant to our ideas of the power, goodness, and foreknowledge of the Deity.

It cannot be considered as an unimproving exercise of the human mind to endeavour to "Vindicate the ways of God to man" if we proceed with a proper distrust of our own understandings and a just sense of our insufficiency to comprehend the reason of all that we see, if we hail every ray of light with gratitude, and when no light appears, think that the darkness is from within and not from without, and bow with humble deference to the supreme wisdom of him whose "thoughts are above our thoughts" "as the heavens are high above the earth."

In all our feeble attempts, however, to "find out the Almighty to perfection," it seems absolutely necessary that we should reason from nature up to nature's God and not presume to reason from God to nature. The moment we allow ourselves to ask why some things are not otherwise, instead of endeavouring to account for them as they are, we shall never know where to stop, we shall be led into the grossest and most childish absurdities, all progress in the knowledge of the ways of Providence must necessarily be at an end, and the study will even cease to be an improving exercise of the human mind. Infinite power is so vast and incomprehensible an idea that the mind of man must necessarily be bewildered in the contemplation of it. With the crude and puerile conceptions which we sometimes form of this attribute of the Deity, we might imagine that God could call into being myriads and myriads of existences, all free from pain and imperfection, all eminent in goodness and wisdom, all capable of the highest enjoyments, and unnumbered as the points throughout infinite space. But when from these vain and extravagant dreams of fancy, we turn our eyes to the book of nature, where alone we can read God as he is, we see a constant succession of sentient beings, rising apparently from so many specks of matter, going through a long and sometimes painful process in this world, but many of them attaining, ere the termination of it, such high qualities and powers as seem to indicate their fitness for some superior state. Ought we not then to correct our crude and puerile ideas of Infinite Power from the contemplation of what we actually see existing? Can we judge of the Creator but from his creation? And, unless we wish to exalt the power of God at the expence of his goodness, ought we not to conclude that even to the Great Creator, Almighty as he is, a certain process may be necessary, a certain time (or at least what appears to us as time) may be requisite, in order to form beings with those exalted qualities of mind which will fit them for his high purposes?

A state of trial seems to imply a previously formed existence that does not agree with the appearance of man in infancy and indicates something like suspicion and want of foreknowledge, inconsistent with those ideas which we wish to cherish of the Supreme Being. I should be inclined, therefore, as I have hinted before in a note, to consider the world and this life as the mighty process of God, not for the trial, but for the creation and formation of mind, a process necessary to awaken inert, chaotic matter into spirit, to sublimate the dust of the earth into soul, to elicit an ethereal spark from the clod of clay. And in this view of the subject, the various impressions and excitements which man receives through life may be considered as the forming hand of his Creator, acting by general laws, and awakening his sluggish existence, by the animating touches of the Divinity, into a capacity of superior enjoyment. The original sin of man is the torpor and corruption of the chaotic matter in which he may be said to be born.

It could answer no good purpose to enter into the question whether mind be a distinct substance from matter, or only a finer form of it. The question is, perhaps, after all, a question merely of words. Mind is as essentially mind, whether formed from matter or any other substance. We know from experience that soul and body are most intimately united, and every appearance seems to indicate that they grow from infancy together. It would be a supposition attended with very little probability to believe that a complete and full formed spirit existed in every infant, but that it was clogged and impeded in its operations during the first twenty years of life by the weakness, or hebetude, of the organs in which it was enclosed. As we shall all be disposed to agree that God is the creator of mind as well as of body, and as they both seem to be forming and unfolding themselves at the same time, it cannot appear inconsistent either with reason or revelation, if it appear to be consistent with phenomena of nature, to suppose that God is constantly occupied in forming mind out of matter and that the various impressions that man receives through life is the process for that purpose. The employment is surely worthy of the highest attributes of the Deity.

This view of the state of man on earth will not seem to be unattended with probability, if, judging from the little experience we have of the nature of mind, it shall appear upon investigation that the phenomena around us, and the various events of human life, seem peculiarly calculated to promote this great end, and especially if, upon this supposition, we can account, even to our own narrow understandings, for many of those roughnesses and inequalities in life which querulous man too frequently makes the subject of his complaint against the God of nature.

The first great awakeners of the mind seem to be the wants of the body.* They are the first stimulants that rouse the brain of infant man into sentient activity, and such seems to be the sluggishness of original matter that unless by a peculiar course of excitements other wants, equally powerful, are generated, these stimulants seem, even afterwards, to be necessary to continue that activity which they first awakened. The savage would slumber for ever under his tree unless he were roused from his torpor by the cravings of hunger or the pinchings of cold, and the exertions that he makes to avoid these evils, by procuring food, and building himself a covering, are the exercises which form and keep in motion his faculties, which otherwise would sink into listless inactivity. From all that experience has taught us concerning the structure of the human mind, if those stimulants to exertion, which arise from the wants of the body, were removed from the mass of mankind, we have much more reason to think that they would be sunk to the level of brutes, from a deficiency of excitements, than that they would be raised to the rank of philosophers by the possession of leisure. In those countries where nature is the most redundant in spontaneous produce the inhabitants will not be found the most remarkable for acuteness of intellect. Necessity has been with great truth called the mother of invention. Some of the noblest exertions of the human mind have been set in motion by the necessity of satisfying the wants of the body. Want has not unfrequently given wings to the imagination of the poet, pointed the flowing periods of the historian, and added acuteness to the researches of the philosopher, and though there are undoubtedly many minds at present so far improved by the various excitements of knowledge, or of social sympathy that they would not relapse into listlessness, if their bodily stimulants were removed, yet it can scarcely be doubted that these stimulants could not be withdrawn from the mass of mankind without producing a general and fatal torpor, destructive of all the germs of future improvement.

Locke, if I recollect, says that the endeavour to avoid pain

---

* It was my intention to have entered at some length into this subject as a kind of second part to the essay. A long interruption, from particular business, has obliged me to lay aside this intention, at least for the present. I shall now, therefore, only give a sketch of a few of the leading circumstances that appear to me to favour the general supposition that I have advanced.

rather than the pursuit of pleasure is the great stimulus to action in life: and that in looking to any particular pleasure, we shall not be roused into action in order to obtain it, till the contemplation of it has continued so long as to amount to a sensation of pain or uneasiness under the absence of it. To avoid evil and to pursue good seem to be the great duty and business of man, and this world appears to be peculiarly calculated to afford opportunity of the most unremitted exertion of this kind, and it is by this exertion, by these stimulants, that mind is formed. If Locke's idea be just, and there is great reason to think that it is, evil seems to be necessary to create exertion, and exertion seems evidently necessary to create mind.

The necessity of food for the support of life gives rise, probably, to a greater quantity of exertion than any other want, bodily or mental. The supreme Being has ordained that the earth shall not produce food in great quantities till much preparatory labour and ingenuity has been exercised upon its surface. There is no conceivable connection to our comprehensions, between the seed and the plant or tree that rises from it. The Supreme Creator might, undoubtedly, raise up plants of all kinds, for the use of his creatures without the assistance of those little bits of matter, which we call seed, or even without the assisting labour and attention of man. The processes of ploughing and clearing the ground, of collecting and sowing seeds, are not surely for the assistance of God in his creation, but are made previously necessary to the enjoyment of the blessings of life, in order to rouse man into action, and form his mind to reason.

To furnish the most unremitted excitements of this kind, and to urge man to further the gracious designs of Providence, by the full cultivation of the earth, it has been ordained that population should increase much faster than food. This general law (as it has appeared in the former parts of this essay) undoubtedly produces much partial evil, but a little reflection may, perhaps, satisfy us, that it produces a great overbalance of good. Strong excitements seem necessary to create exertion, and to direct this exertion, and form the reasoning faculty, it seems absolutely necessary, that the Supreme Being should act always according to general laws. The constancy of the laws of nature, or the certainty, with which we may expect the same effect, from the same causes, is the foundation of the faculty of reason. If in the ordinary course of things, the finger of God were frequently visible, or to speak more correctly, if God were frequently to change his purpose (for the finger of God is, indeed, visible in every blade of grass that we see), a general and fatal torpor of the human faculties would probably ensue, even the bodily wants of mankind would cease to stimulate them to exertion, could they not reasonably expect that if their efforts were well directed they would be crowned with success. The constancy of the laws of nature, is the foundation of the industry and foresight of the husbandman, the indefatigable ingenuity of the artificer, the skilful researches of the physician and anatomist, and the watchful observation and patient investigation of the natural philosopher. To this constancy we owe all the greatest and noblest efforts of intellect. To this constancy we owe the immortal mind of a Newton.

As the reasons, therefore, for the constancy of the laws of nature, seem, even to our understandings, obvious and striking, if we return to the principle of population and consider man as he really is, inert, sluggish, and averse from labour, unless compelled by necessity (and it is surely the height of folly to talk of man, according to our crude fancies, of what he might be), we may pronounce with certainty that the world would not have been peopled, but for the superiority of the power of population to the means of subsistence. Strong and constantly operative as this stimulus is on man to urge him to the cultivation of the earth, if we still see that cultivation proceeds very slowly, we may fairly conclude that a less stimulus would have been insufficient. Even under the operation of this constant excitement, savages will inhabit countries of the greatest natural fertility for a long period before they betake themselves to pasturage or agriculture. Had population and food increased in the same ratio, it is probable that man might never have emerged from the savage state. But supposing the earth once well peopled, an Alexander. a Julius Caesar, a Tamerlane, or a bloody revolution might irrecoverably thin the human race, and defeat the great designs of the Creator. The ravages of a contagious disorder would be felt for ages; and an earthquake might unpeople a region for ever. The principle, according to which population increases, prevents the vices of mankind, or the accidents of nature, the partial evils arising from general laws, from obstructing the high purpose of the creation. It keeps the inhabitants of the earth always fully up to the level of the means of subsistence; and is constantly acting upon man as a powerful stimulus, urging him to the further cultivation of the earth, and to enable it, consequently, to support a more extended population. But it is impossible that this law can operate, and produce the effects apparently intended by the Supreme Being, without occasioning partial evil. Unless the principle of population were to be altered, according to the circumstances of each separate country (which would not only be contrary to our universal experience, with regard to the laws of nature, but would contradict even our own reason, which sees the absolute necessity of general laws, for the formation of intellect), it is evident that the same principle which, seconded by industry, will people a fertile region in a few years must produce distress in countries that have been long inhabited.

It seems, however, every way probable that even the acknowledged difficulties occasioned by the law of population, tend rather to promote than impede the general purpose of Providence. They excite universal exertion and contribute to that infinite variety of situations, and consequently of impressions, which seems upon the whole favourable to the growth of mind. It is probable, that too great or too little excitement, extreme poverty, or too great riches may be alike unfavourable in this respect. The middle regions of society seem to be best suited to intellectual improvement, but it is contrary to the analogy of all nature, to expect that the whole of society can be a middle region. The temperate zones of the earth seem to be the most favourable to the mental and corporeal energies of man, but all cannot be temperate zones. A world, warmed and enlightened but by one sun, must from the laws of matter have some parts chilled by perpetual frosts and others scorched by perpetual heats. Every piece of matter lying on a surface must have an upper and an under side, all the particles cannot be in the middle. The most valuable parts of an oak, to a timber merchant, are not either the roots or the branches, but these are absolutely necessary to the existence of the middle part, or stem, which is the object in request. The timber merchant could not possibly expect to make an oak grow without roots or branches, but if he could find out a mode of cultivation which would cause more of the substance to go to stem, and less to root and branch, he would be right to exert himself in bringing such a system into general use.

In the same manner, though we cannot possibly expect to exclude riches and poverty from society, yet if we could find out a mode of government by which the numbers in the extreme regions would be lessened and the numbers in the middle regions increased, it would be undoubtedly our duty to adopt it. It is not, however, improbable that as in the oak, the roots and branches could not be diminished very greatly without weakening the vigorous circulation of the sap in the stem, so in society the extreme parts could not be diminished beyond a certain degree without lessening that animated exertion throughout the middle parts, which is the very cause that they are the most favourable to the growth of intellect. If no man could hope to rise or fear to fall, in society, if industry did not bring with it its reward and idleness its punishment, the middle parts would not certainly be what they now are. In reasoning upon this subject, it is evident that we ought to consider chiefly the mass of mankind and not individual instances. There are undoubtedly many minds, and there ought to be many, according to the chances, out of so great a mass that, having been vivified early by a peculiar course of excitements, would not need the constant action of narrow motives to continue them in activity. But if we were to review the various useful discoveries, the valuable writings, and other laudable exertions of mankind, I believe we should find that more were to be attributed to the narrow motives that operate upon the many than to the apparently more enlarged motives that operate upon upon the few.

Leisure is, without doubt, highly valuable to man, but taking man as he is, the probability seems to be that in the greater number of instances it will produce evil rather than good. It has been not unfrequently remarked that talents are more common among younger brothers than among elder brothers, but it can scarcely be imagined that younger brothers are, upon an average, born with a greater original susceptibility of parts. The difference, if there really is any observable difference, can only arise from their different situations. Exertion and activity are in general absolutely necessary in the one case and are only optional in the other.

That the difficulties of life contribute to generate talents, every day's experience must convince us. The exertions that men find it necessary to make, in order to support themselves or families, frequently awaken faculties, that might otherwise have lain for ever dormant, and it has been commonly remarked that new and extraordinary situations generally create minds adequate to grapple with the difficulties in which they are involved.

CHAPTER XIX

The sorrows and distresses of life form another class of excitements, which seem to be necessary, by a peculiar train of impressions, to soften and humanize the heart, to awaken social sympathy, to generate all the Christian virtues, and to afford scope for the ample exertion of benevolence. The general tendency of an uniform course of prosperity is rather to degrade than exalt the character. The heart that has never known sorrow itself will seldom be feelingly alive to the pains and pleasures, the wants and wishes, of its fellow beings. It will seldom be overflowing with that warmth of brotherly love, those kind and amiable affections, which dignify the human character even more than the possession of the highest talents. Talents, indeed, though undoubtedly a very prominent and fine feature of mind, can by no means be considered as constituting the whole of it. There are many minds which have not been exposed to those excitements that usually form talents, that have yet been vivified to a high degree by the excitements of social sympathy. In every rank of life, in the lowest as frequently as in the highest, characters are to be found overflowing with the milk of human kindness, breathing love towards God and man, and though without those peculiar powers of mind called talents, evidently holding a higher rank in the scale of beings than many who possess them. Evangelical charity, meekness, piety, and all that class of virtues distinguished particularly by the name of Christian virtues do not seem necessarily to include abilities, yet a soul possessed of these amiable qualities, a soul awakened and vivified by these delightful sympathies, seems to hold a nearer commerce with the skies than mere acuteness of intellect.

The greatest talents have been frequently misapplied and have produced evil proportionate to the extent of their powers. Both reason and revelation seem to assure us that such minds will be condemned to eternal death, but while on earth, these vicious instruments performed their part in the great mass of impressions, by the disgust and abhorrence which they excited. It seems highly probable, that moral evil is absolutely necessary to the production of moral excellence. A being with only good placed in view, may be justly said to be impelled by a blind necessity. The pursuit of good in this case can be no indication of virtuous propensities. It might be said, perhaps, that Infinite Wisdom cannot want such an indication as outward action, but would foreknow with certainty whether the being would chuse good or evil. This might be a plausible argument against a state of trial, but will not hold against the supposition that mind in this world is in a state of formation. Upon this idea, the being that has seen moral evil and has felt disapprobation and disgust at it is essentially different from the being that has seen only good. They are pieces of clay that have received distinct impressions: they must, therefore, necessarily be in different shapes; or, even if we allow them both to have the same lovely form of virtue, it must be acknowledged, that one has undergone the further process, necessary to give firmness and durability to its substance; while the other is still exposed to injury, and liable to be broken by every accidental impulse. An ardent love and admiration of virtue seems to imply the existence of something opposite to it, and it seems highly probable that the same beauty of form and substance, the same perfection of character, could not be generated without the impressions of disapprobation which arise from the spectacle of moral evil.

When the mind has been awakened into activity by the passions, and the wants of the body, intellectual wants arise; and the desire of knowledge, and the impatience under ignorance, form a new and important class of excitements. Every part of nature seems peculiarly calculated to furnish stimulants to mental exertion of this kind, and to offer inexhaustible food for the most unremitted inquiry. Our immortal Bard says of Cleopatra—

> Custom cannot stale
> Her infinite variety.

the expression, when applied to any one object, may be considered
as a poetical amplification, but it is accurately true when applied
to nature. Infinite variety, seems, indeed, eminently her character-
istic feature. The shades that are here and there blended in the
picture give spirit, life, and prominence to her exuberant beauties,
and those roughnesses and inequalities, those inferior parts that
support the superior, though they sometimes offend the fastidious
microscopic eye of short sighted man, contribute to the symmetry,
grace, and fair proportion of the whole.

The infinite variety of the forms and operations of nature,
besides tending immediately to awaken and improve the mind
by the variety of impressions that it creates, opens other fertile
sources of improvement by offering so wide and extensive a field
for investigation and research. Uniform, undiversified perfection
could not possess the same awakening powers. When we endeavour then to contemplate the system of the universe, when we think
of the stars as the suns of other systems scattered throughout
infinite space, when we reflect that we do not probably see a mil-
lionth part of those bright orbs that are beaming light and life to
unnumbered worlds, when our minds unable to grasp the immeasurable conception sink, lost and confounded, in admiration
at the mighty incomprehensible power of the Creator, let us not
querulously complain that all climates are not equally genial, that
perpetual spring does not reign throughout the year, that all
God's creatures do not possess the same advantages, that clouds
and tempests sometimes darken the natural world and vice and
misery the moral world, and that all the works of the creation are
not formed with equal perfection. Both reason and experience
seem to indicate to us that the infinite variety of nature (and
variety cannot exist without inferior parts, or apparent blemishes)
is admirably adapted to further the high purpose of the creation
and to produce the greatest possible quantity of good.

The obscurity that involves all metaphysical subjects appears
to me, in the same manner peculiarly calculated, to add to that
class of excitements which arise from the thirst of knowledge. It
is probable that man, while on earth, will never be able to attain
complete satisfaction on these subjects; but this is by no means a
reason that he should not engage in them. The darkness that

surrounds these interesting topics of human curiosity, may be intended to furnish endless motives to intellectual activity and exertion. The constant effort to dispel this darkness, even if it fail of success, invigorates and improves the thinking faculty. If the subjects of human inquiry were once exhausted, mind would probably stagnate; but the infinitely diversified forms and operations of nature, together with the endless food for speculation which metaphysical subjects offer, prevent the possibility that such a period should ever arrive.

It is by no means one of the wisest sayings of Solomon that "there is no new thing under the sun." On the contrary, it is probable that were the present system to continue for millions of years, continual additions would be making to the mass of human knowledge, and yet, perhaps, it may be a matter of doubt whether what may be called the capacity of mind be in any marked and decided manner increasing. A Socrates, a Plato, or an Aristotle, however confessedly inferior in knowledge to the philosophers of the present day, do not appear to have been much below them in intellectual capacity. Intellect rises from a speck, continues in vigour only for a certain period, and will not perhaps admit while on earth of above a certain number of impressions. These impressions may, indeed, be infinitely modified, and from these various modifications, added probably to a difference in the susceptibility of the original germs,* arise the endless diversity of character that we see in the world; but reason and experience seem both to assure us, that the capacity of individual minds does not increase in proportion to the mass of existing knowledge. The finest minds seem to be formed rather by efforts at original thinking, by endeavours to form new combinations, and to discover new truths, than by passively receiving the impressions of other men's ideas. Could we suppose the period arrived, when there was no further hope of future discoveries; and the only employment of mind was to acquire pre-existing knowledge, without any efforts to form

---

* It is probable that no two grains of wheat are exactly alike. Soil undoubtedly makes the principal difference in the blades that spring up, but probably not all. It seems natural to suppose some sort of difference in the original germs that are afterwards awakened into thought, and the extraordinary difference of susceptibility in very young children seems to confirm the supposition.

new and original combinations; though the mass of human knowledge were a thousand times greater than it is at present; yet it is evident that one of the noblest stimulants to mental exertion would have ceased; the finest feature of intellect would be lost; every thing allied to genius would be at an end; and it appears to be impossible, that, under such circumstances, any individuals could possess the same intellectual energies, as were possessed by a Locke, a Newton, or a Shakespear, or even by a Socrates, a Plato, an Aristotle, or a Homer.

If a revelation from heaven of which no person could feel the smallest doubt were to dispel the mists that now hang over metaphysical subjects, were to explain the nature and structure of mind, the affections and essences of all substances, the mode in which the Supreme Being operates in the works of the creation, and the whole plan and scheme of the Universe, such an accession of knowledge so obtained, instead of giving additional vigour and activity to the human mind, would in all probability tend to repress future exertion and to damp the soaring wings of intellect.

For this reason I have never considered the doubts and difficulties that involve some parts of the sacred writings, as any argument against their divine original. The Supreme Being might, undoubtedly, have accompanied his revelations to man by such a succession of miracles, and of such a nature, as would have produced universal overpowering conviction and have put an end at once to all hesitation and discussion. But weak as our reason is to comprehend the plans of the Great Creator, it is yet sufficiently strong to see the most striking objections to such a revelation. From the little we know of the structure of the human understanding, we must be convinced that an overpowering conviction of this kind, instead of tending to the improvement and moral amelioration of man, would act like the touch of a torpedo on all intellectual exertion and would almost put at end to the existence of virtue. If the scriptural denunciations of eternal punishment were brought home with the same certainty to every man's mind as that the night will follow the day, this one vast and gloomy idea would take such full possession of the human faculties as to leave no room for any other conceptions, the external actions of men would be all nearly alike, virtuous conduct would be no indication of virtuous disposition, vice and virtue would be blended together in one common mass, and though the all-seeing eye of God might distinguish them they must necessarily make the same impressions on man, who can judge only from external appearances. Under such a dispensation, it is difficult to conceive how human beings could be formed to a detestation of moral evil, and a love and admiration of God, and of moral excellence.

Our ideas of virtue and vice are not, perhaps, very accurate and well-defined; but few, I think, would call an action really virtuous which was performed simply and solely from the dread of a very great punishment or the expectation of a very great reward. The fear of the Lord is very justly said to be the beginning of wisdom, but the end of wisdom is the love of the Lord and the admiration of moral good. The denunciations of future punishment contained in the scriptures seem to be well calculated to arrest the progress of the vicious and awaken the attention of the careless, but we see from repeated experience that they are not accompanied with evidence of such a nature as to overpower the human will and to make men lead virtuous lives with vicious dispositions, merely from a dread of hereafter. A genuine faith, by which I mean a faith that shews itself in all the virtues of a truly christian life, may generally be considered as an indication of an amiable and virtuous disposition, operated upon more by love than by pure unmixed fear.

When we reflect on the temptations to which man must necessarily be exposed in this world, from the structure of his frame, and the operation of the laws of nature, and the consequent moral certainty that many vessels will come out of this mighty creative furnace in wrong shapes, it is perfectly impossible to conceive that any of these creatures of God's hand can be condemned to eternal suffering. Could we once admit such an idea, all our natural conceptions of goodness and justice would be completely overthrown, and we could no longer look up to God as a merciful and righteous Being. But the doctrine of life and immortality which was brought to light by the gospel, the doctrine that the end of righteousness is everlasting life, but that the wages of sin are death, is in every respect just and merciful, and worthy of the Great Creator. Nothing can appear more consonant to our reason than that those beings which come out of the creative process of the world in lovely and beautiful forms, should be crowned with immortality, while those which come out misshapen, those whose minds are not suited to a purer and happier state of existence, should perish and be condemned to mix again with their original clay. Eternal condemnation of this kind may be considered as a species of eternal punishment, and it is not wonderful that it should be represented, sometimes under images of suffering. But life and death, salvation and destruction, are more frequently opposed to each other in the New Testament than happiness and misery. The Supreme Being would appear to us in a very different view if we were to consider him as pursuing the creatures that had offended him with eternal hate and torture, instead of merely condemning to their original insensibility those beings that, by the operation of general laws, had not been formed with qualities suited to a purer state of happiness.

Life is, generally speaking, a blessing independent of a future state. It is a gift which the vicious would not always be ready to throw away, even if they had no fear of death. The partial pain, therefore, that is inflicted by the Supreme Creator, while he is forming numberless beings to a capacity of the highest enjoyments, is but as the dust of the balance in comparison of the happiness that is communicated, and we have every reason to think that there is no more evil in the world than what is absolutely necessary as one of the ingredients in the mighty process.

The striking necessity of general laws for the formation of intellect will not in any respect be contradicted by one or two exceptions, and these evidently not intended for partial purposes, but calculated to operate upon a great part of mankind, and through many ages. Upon the idea that I have given of the formation of mind, the infringement of the general laws of nature, by a divine revelation, will appear in the light of the immediate hand of God mixing new ingredients in the mighty mass, suited to the particular state of the process, and calculated to give rise to a new and powerful train of impressions, tending to purify, exalt, and improve the human mind. The miracles that accompanied these revelations when they had once excited the attention of mankind, and rendered it a matter of most interesting discussion, whether the doctrine was from God or man, had performed their part, had answered the purpose of the Creator; and these communications of the divine will were afterwards left to make their way by their own intrinsic excellence; and by operating as moral motives, gradually to influence and improve, and not to overpower and stagnate the faculties of man.

It would be, undoubtedly, presumptuous to say that the Supreme Being could not possibly have effected his purpose in any other way than that which he has chosen, but as the revelation of the divine will which we possess is attended with some doubts and difficulties, and as our reason points out to us the strongest objections to a revelation which would force immediate, implicit, universal belief, we have surely just cause to think that these doubts and difficulties are no argument against the divine origin of the scriptures, and that the species of evidence which they possess is best suited to the improvement of the human faculties and the moral amelioration of mankind.

The idea that the impressions and excitements of this world are the instruments with which the Supreme Being forms matter into mind, and that the necessity of constant exertion to avoid evil and to pursue good is the principal spring of these impressions and excitements, seems to smooth many of the difficulties that occur in a contemplation of human life, and appears to me to give a satisfactory reason for the existence of natural and moral evil, and, consequently, for that part of both, and it certainly is not a very small part, which arises from the principle of population. But, though upon this supposition, it seems highly improbable that evil should ever be removed from the world, yet it is evident that this impression would not answer the apparent purpose of the Creator, it would not act so powerfully as an excitement to exertion if the quantity of it did not diminish or increase with the activity or the indolence of man. The continual variations in the weight and in the distribution of this pressure keep alive a constant expectation of throwing it off.

> Hope springs eternal in the human breast,
> Man never is, but always to be blest.

Evil exists in the world not to create despair but activity. We are not patiently to submit to it, but to exert ourselves to avoid it.

It is not only the interest but the duty of every individual to use his utmost efforts to remove evil from himself and from as large a circle as he can influence, and the more he exercises himself in this duty, the more wisely he directs his efforts, and the more successful these efforts are, the more he will probably improve and exalt his own mind and the more completely does he appear to fulfil the will of his Creator.

ANN ARBOR PAPERBACKS

reissues of works of enduring merit

The Writer and His Craft
edited by Roy W. Cowden   AA 1

Elizabethan Plays and Players
by G. B. Harrison   AA 2

**The Intellectual Milieu
of John Dryden**
by Louis I. Bredvold   AA 3

The Southern Frontier, 1670–1732
by Verner W. Crane   AA 4

The Concept of Nature
by Alfred North Whitehead   AA 5

Richard Crashaw
by Austin Warren   AA 6

Dialogues in Limbo
by George Santayana   AA 7

The Desert Fathers
by Helen Waddell   AA 8

Stonewall Jackson
by Allen Tate   AA 9

Church, State, and Education
by Sir Ernest Barker   AA 10

Literature and Psychology
by F. L. Lucas   AA 11

**This Was a Poet:
Emily Dickinson**
by George Frisbie Whicher   AA 12

**Thomas Jefferson: The Apostle of
Americanism**
by Gilbert Chinard   AA 13

The Expanding Universe
by Sir Arthur Eddington   AA 14

The Nature of the Physical World
by Sir Arthur Eddington   AA 15

Shakespeare at Work 1592–1603
by G. B. Harrison   AA 16

Six Theosophic Points
by Jacob Boehme   AA 17

Thomas More
by R. W. Chambers   AA 18

Physics and Philosophy
by James Jeans   AA 19

The Philosophy of Physical Science
by Sir Arthur Eddington   AA 20

The Puritan Mind
by Herbert Schneider   AA 21

The Greek View of Life
by G. Lowes Dickinson   AA 22

The Praise of Folly
by Desiderius Erasmus   AA 23

Man's Place in Nature
by Thomas H. Huxley   AA 24

The New Background of Science
by Sir James Jeans   AA 25

Ronsard: Prince of Poets
by Morris Bishop   AA 26

Life in a Noble Household
by Gladys Scott Thomson   AA 27

**Antislavery Origins of the
Civil War**
by Dwight Lowell Dumond   AA 28

New Pathways in Science
by Sir Arthur Eddington   AA 29

Devotions
by John Donne   AA 30

Population: The First Essay
by Thomas R. Malthus   AA 31

The Song of Roland
Translated by C. K. Scott Moncrieff   AA 32

Rage for Order
by Austin Warren   AA 33

The University of Michigan Press | Ann Arbor